Bayou SALADO
THE STORY OF SOUTH PARK
REVISED EDITION

VIRGINIA McCONNELL SIMMONS

UNIVERSITY PRESS OF COLORADO

Published by the University Press of Colorado
5589 Arapahoe Avenue, Suite 206C
Boulder, Colorado 80303

The University Press of Colorado is a cooperative publishing enterprise supported, in part, by Adams State College, Colorado State University, Fort Lewis College, Mesa State College, Metropolitan State College of Denver, University of Colorado, University of Northern Colorado, University of Southern Colorado, and Western State College of Colorado.

The paper used in this publication meets the minimum requirements of the American National Standard for Information Sciences—Permanence of Paper for Printed Library Materials. ANSI Z39.48-1992

Library of Congress Cataloging-in-Publication Data

Simmons, Virginia McConnell, 1928–
    Bayou Salado : the story of South Park / by Virginia McConnell Simmons.
        p. cm.
    Includes bibliographical references and index.
    ISBN 0-87081-670-5 (alk. paper)
    1. South Park (Colo.)—History. I. Title.

F782.S6 S55 2002
978.8'59—dc21

                                                    200218119

Cover design by Daniel Pratt

11   10   09   08   07   10 9 8 7 6 5 4 3 2

For Tom and Susie,

and for Abby Kernochan who knew the promised land.

ALSO BY VIRGINIA McCONNELL SIMMONS

Ute Pass: Route of the Blue Sky People

The Springs of Manitou (with Bettie Marie Daniels)

The San Luis Valley:
Land of the Six Armed Cross, Second Edition

Valley of the Cranes

The Upper Arkansas

The Ute Indians of Utah, Colorado, and New Mexico

FOREWORD

The reissue of *Bayou Salado: The Story of South Park* thirty-six years after its first appearance confirms a suspicion that some books, like offspring, take on lives of their own and strike off in directions not anticipated at the time of their birth. Originally published by Sage Books, Fred Pruett Books gave this book the chance to continue its stubborn career long after it might have retired and allowed for the addition of a new map, drafted by my husband, geologist George C. Simmons.

The continued interest in this slice of Colorado's story is gratifying to me, because I have an abiding faith in the value of regional history. Whether or not our lives have been entwined with a place like South Park, we become enriched by remembering the people who lived and worked there in previous times. Those individuals were real people with hands and minds and purposes like our own, although their place and age posed different problems and offered different opportunities. By reading about them we expand our own lives, our own range of imagination, and our own potential. We also understand better the meaning of broader histories and may even be able to say sometimes, "But there was more to the story than that."

To look at a breathtakingly beautiful landscape like South Park and to visualize events that occurred gives me pleasure. Apparently, it pleases other people, too, for more and more people are discovering South Park. Although the rapid growth of population along Colorado's Front Range accounts in part for this increase in tourism, the rising cost of transportation will continue to make South Park a desirable place to escape from the pressures of life in nearby cities.

It is hoped that this new printing of *Bayou Salado* will help visitors and residents enjoy and understand the unique place that is called South Park. It is hoped, too, that in appreciating its beauty and history, people will be encouraged to preserve those qualities.

One needs no special sensibilities to feel a sudden choke of wonder when he looks for the first time down across the immense upland valley of South Park—beyond the clumps of straw-dry grass and glittering chunks of mica and granite at his feet, beyond the quivering aspens which patch the hills on either side with gold.

Beyond them, the hazy, grey-beige valley seems suspended on the surface of some weightless mirage. Here and there islands, blackened with ragged shawls of pine and fir, jut up from the shimmering monotone of earth. Fifty miles or so away sharp crystalline peaks rim the edge, cupping the land lest it spill out and drift away.

And above and above, deep, palpable, the dome-sky spreads across the land. Only the blue, the incredible blue of the sky, seems tangible. A canopy, it is the one element which seems to hold this strange, waiting dream against the earth.

Table of Contents

Table of Illustrations

CHAPTER ONE

The Virgin Land

If ever there was a land of subtle, magnetic charms, South Park is that place. Rich in beauty, sparkling rivers, game, mineral wealth, range land, and legend, the valley and its ring of mountains have held the promise of fulfillment to all who have come there through the centuries. This magical place has seldom failed them. Instead, the caprice and frailty of the men themselves have led to the occasional disappointments that the park has witnessed. That South Park's resources have outlasted man's effort to exploit them is part of its mystical allure.

Today South Park attracts another kind of searcher, too. Here in the heart of the Rockies, accessible to travel, yet remote enough to be spared modern man's defacement of its virgin beauty, the park beckons him to make peace with his twentieth-century restlessness and neuroses. The gentleness and the savagery alike of this unspoiled land speak to a fundamental need of our new searcher, our civilized man who cannot find himself, lost in a journey among his own endeavors.

There is a certain perverse comfort in knowing that this magnificent land, like man, is not eternal. In that sense the park becomes a challenge to him to accept its beauty and dimension and resources on terms that he can recognize in human life and perhaps can weave into his own creations.

And so to South Park . . .

From Wilkerson Pass one sees a large portion of the park

spread out in its startling immensity. Coming to this pass the traveler has wound up through the wooded hills of the Front Range, past the great, bald mass of Pikes Peak which now looms behind to the east.

Far across South Park on the west side lie the white alkaline marshes and salt springs to which the Indians once came while following game. The Spaniards called the park *Valle Salado,* or Salt Valley, when they passed through. French explorers and trappers, also intrigued by the saline ground and springs, later used the Creole name *Bayou Salade,* Salt Marshes. But the American mountain men gave the valley their own hybrid title by calling it the *Bayou Salado,* a name which became the synonym of romance, adventure, and fortune to the American trapper.

The name South Park was first used in the 1840's when a chain of large mountain valleys—North Park, Middle Park, South Park, and to a lesser extent the San Luis Valley—were becoming a popular circuit for American hunters. Since these valleys were the feeding grounds of vast herds of game, the word *park* was used to describe the regions, the French word for a game preserve being *parc.*

This chain of parks runs down through the center of Colorado like spaces between the vertebrae of the mountains; and South Park is located in the very center of the state. It is a large plateau, fifty miles long and thirty-five miles wide, bordered on all sides by mountains. Although the flat land of the park occupies 900 square miles, there are 1,400 square miles within the circumference of the surrounding peaks. The floor of the basin varies from 8,500 feet to 10,000 feet above sea level.

Whereas the mountains around Wilkerson Pass and to the south are relatively low, not rising above timberline, the snow-capped peaks to the north and northwest soar to 13,000 and 14,000 feet or more. These high, glistening summits were called the Snowy Range by the trappers and by the goldseekers of the 1860's. Burt and Berthoud, who prepared a guidebook for the early gold rush emigrants, described the Snowy Range as running easterly between the South and Middle Parks, then north to

14

Longs Peak, and eventually on up the west side of North Park. Later on, the name "Park Range" was substituted for the entire rambling chain of peaks, but "Park Range" now is applied only to two widely separated groups of mountains—those on the north edge of South Park and those in the vicinity of North Park.

The Park Range extending from Kenosha Pass and Red Cone to Hoosier Pass defines the northern rim of South Park. The range lies on the Continental Divide for the most part and runs on a cross-grain to the other high uplifts of the Central Rockies. Beautifully symmetrical, Mt. Silverheels, named for a dance hall girl, juts out into the park from the lofty ridge of peaks.

The mountains lying south of Hoosier Pass and along the west side of South Park are now known as the Mosquito Range. The Mosquitoes are not part of the Continental Divide, although the height of the summits near Fairplay might lead one to believe that they are. The northern Mosquitoes include five peaks over 14,000 feet—Mounts Lincoln, Cameron, Bross, Democrat, and Sherman—as well as twenty or so above 13,000 feet. Mosquito Pass is the highest in the country crossed by a road today. Into the deeply carved valleys and up the jagged sides of the Mosquitoes swarmed the miners looking for a vault of treasure. And they found many, even naming one summit Treasurevault Mountain in awe.

The Mosquitoes south of Trout Creek Pass are all below timberline, including the highest in the group, Cameron Mountain (not to be confused with the skyscraper Mount Cameron). The whole Mosquito Range separates South Park from the valley of the Arkansas River to the west.

Most of the Mosquito Range rose about 600 million years ago. However, the two snowy humps of the Buffalo Peaks, midway down the range and just north of Trout Creek Pass, are volcanic piles which were created after the Mosquito uplift.

The hills across the southern end of the park are reminiscent of the wooded ridges of the Green Mountains of Vermont. However, the benign aspect of Big Black Mountain and Thirtynine Mile Mountain cloaks an often dark history of rustlers, outlaws, and madmen.

These southern hills were created by volcanic activity which centered around Guffey south of the park. The volcanic ridges and lava dams blocked the Middle Fork of the South Platte River from flowing south to the Arkansas River and diverted it through the Front Range. With headwaters in the Mosquito Range in the northwestern corner of the park, the Platte is South Park's major water drainage with its own two forks—the South Fork and the Middle Fork which join near Hartsel. The Platte has cut an outlet from the southeast corner of the park through Elevenmile Canyon.

North of Elevenmile Canyon the Puma Hills separate South Park from the Front Range and the nearby Tarryall Mountains. Tarryall Creek flows down between the Puma Hills and the Tarryall Mountains, carrying the waters that drain the northeast portion of the park. This stream joins the Platte in the hills of the Front Range.

The Puma Hills, dominated by Badger Mountain to the north of Wilkerson Pass, is a later formation than the other uplifts of South Park; but it was one of the major thrust faults of the Rockies, and it brought up the underlying Precambrian sediments, lavas, and intrusive rocks. These rocks became the schists and gneisses which sparkle on Wilkerson Pass, giving a false illusion of gold dust at one's feet.

About midway across the park's basin one sees a low, pine-clad ridge, a Dakota Hogback formation which is called Red Hill. Running north and south, Red Hill bisects South Park. It is broken by two water gaps where the Middle and South Forks of the Platte cut through. These gaps, especially the one at Hartsel, provided natural routes across the park.

The floor of South Park is sometimes spoken of as a peneplain, a flat surface appearing at an elevation of about 9,000 feet among the mountains of central Colorado. Another explanation is that the floor of South Park is a deposit basin. Upon this floor terraces, moraines, and additional deposits have accumulated from volcanic and glacial flows. The glacial deposits are most in evidence in the northwest portion where the Wisconsin Moraine and Plain just west of Fairplay have been dredged for gold. The deeply carved slopes of the Mosquitoes and cirques such as Horseshoe Mountain's contributed to these deposits in relatively late periods of erosion. Pumice and volcanic tuff, in the meantime, washed down in the south-central area.

This basin became through the centuries a great sweep of grassland, threaded with the sparkling streams of the Platte and the Tarryall with their tributaries. Muted, mostly level, it is thought by some to be monotonous. By others it is thought to be a majestic stage for the pageant of history that has crossed it.

Not much imagination is required to visualize the large, varied animal herds and colonies that abounded before man came to the *Bayou Salado.* There were once found buffalo and antelope grazing in vast herds. Ducks, geese, beaver, muskrat, otter, mink, and trout inhabited the waterways. Grizzly bear, Bighorn sheep, wolf, mule deer, elk, and cougar moved through the timbered slopes of the mountains. It was this superb hunting ground that the Ute Indians prized above all others and fought to hold against invading tribes.

Hundreds of buffalo, the largest of the wild animals of North America, were found around the springs and sloughs. Although the buffalo, the bison of the mountains, were somewhat smaller than those of the plains, the bulls were often six feet high at the shoulder and weighed a ton. As they moved with the seasons from one range to another, even from the plains to the mountains and back in some instances, the lush grasslands of the parks, especially South Park, provided summer pasture. The Utes, much like the Plains Indians in culture, followed the immense beasts which had become a self-contained supply of all of the necessities of life for the Indian.

Originally bison inhabited all of the area now in the United States east of the Rockies to the Atlantic and north of Georgia, but by 1800 the herds were found predominantly in the Mountain States area and on the high plains. In the middle 1840's the bison were gone from the prairies immediately east of the Rockies, but they still ranged the mountain parks. George Frederick Ruxton reported in 1847 that the buffalo had disappeared from the fort at the site of Pueblo, but he saw many buffalo skulls and bones.

He went on to comment that the animals still were to be found "particularly . . . in Bayou Salado."

The Indians and natural enemies, such as predators, drouth, or snow, diminished the buffalo from time to time, but the herds were abruptly killed off within a few years after white settlement. The building of the Union Pacific across the West in 1868 made buffalo hunting profitable with access to markets. Furthermore, the whites found the removal of the Indians' sustenance an effective means of bringing the "savages" to bay. By 1874 the buffalo south of the Union Pacific were nearly extinct.

However, tiny remnants were hidden away in remote areas. Reportedly, the last of the wild buffalo in Colorado were killed in 1897 when four were shot in Lost Park, an isolated valley which runs out of South Park in its northeast corner. Since the hunting of buffalo had been closed by law in Colorado in 1877, the discovery of the hides at a cabin resulted in some unpleasant publicity for the culprits as well as the confiscation of the hides. However, the buffalo slaughter story still was not complete, for three of them were killed in 1960 on a modern, main highway east of Hartsel. A domestic herd from the Hartsel Ranch had torn down a fence and milled onto the road where they were struck by cars.

The pronghorn antelope also lived on the park's grassland, often in the same range with the buffalo. In the mid-1880's the number of antelope approximated that of the buffalo. The antelope had two natural protections—one being speed, for they could run as fast as fifty miles an hour; the other being their white rump patches which served as warning to others when the hairs were raised in flight. Also, the antelope could escape into rougher country than could the buffalo. It is said that Indians did not eat antelope meat unless necessary, a fact which further aided the animal's survival.

Today antelope are often seen in South Park from Hartsel east to Wilkerson Pass, about 1,000 animals being in the park. Brown and white and weighing only about 100 pounds, they are distinguished by two white bands under the neck and by short, pronged horns. These horns are unlike antlers in that only the

18

outer sheaths are shed annually while the bony core of the horn is permanent.

But it was the beaver which drew trappers to the park and which made its name known east of the Rockies. Beaver changed dramatically the history of the West, and South Park with it. The largest rodent of North America, the beaver is over a yard long, including his broad, flat tail, and weighs from thirty to sixty pounds. Thus, he has a good-sized pelt. Beneath stiff outer hairs the beaver has a soft under-fur of rich brown.

Any place in the mountains that there were enough water and trees to build a dam, the beaver could be found. He thrived in the valleys of the Mosquito and Park ranges where he built his house of sticks and mud in the water or burrowed into a bank. In either case the entrance was beneath the water's surface. The dam ensured water deep enough for an entry below the winter's ice covering. The smart whack of his tail on the water is his warning to other beaver that intruders are nearby, and the sound still is a familiar one to fishermen around the beaver ponds that lace South Park's mountain valleys.

Perhaps the least romantic but most prevalent of the park's animals was the prairie dog. Where once there were hundreds of villages, now only a few remain. In the 1940's a plague killed about ninety-five per cent of the prairie dogs, which previously had been continuous over the entire park. The Wyoming ground squirrel, which are found in the mountains and in the timber near the edge of the grassland, made a come-back after the plague, but the prairie dog did not.

Bighorn, or Rocky Mountain, sheep still can be found bounding across talus slopes on the mountains. Although the herd in the Tarryall Mountains is well known to be one of the largest in the United States, the one in the southern Mosquito Range is even larger. Grass is the principal food, but the sheep also browse on such shrubs as willow and cinquefoil. As the herds have become increasingly concentrated into small isolated areas, however, lack of sufficient food has weakened the animals and made them vulnerable to disease, especially lungworm, or pneumonia.

During the winter of 1952-53, 150 animals died in the Tarryall herd alone.

The grizzly bear, once fairly common, now are gone. Ruxton reported that the mountains were full of them, although they seemed to be in hibernation at the time of his report. Nevertheless, he claimed to have followed the track of one into *Bayou Salado*, where he still saw no bear but about 100 elk. The elk is found chiefly around the Buffalo Peaks today, but deer are more widespread.

South Park was a hunter's paradise, and large groups of big game hunters began to come after the trophies in the mid-1800's. Undoubtedly, the most elaborate of all of these outfits was the party of Sir George Gore, an Irish peer for whom the Gore Range was named. In 1855, with mountain man Jim Bridger as his guide, Gore hunted in South Park during a two-year tour of the West. Gore had with him fifty servants, thirty supply wagons, and enough hunting dogs to ensure success.

In the early years of white settlement, commercial hunting was carried on in South Park to supply markets in mining towns and in communities east of the mountains. There was so much game that often only the best cuts were sent to market. During the summer two horse-loads of ducks might be taken out in a day. However, by 1870 commercial hunting had nearly ended in the park with the availability of beef cattle.

Occasionally efforts were made to create a game preserve in South Park, and as early as the 1890's Lost Park was made one. In the 1930's the Isaak Walton League was fostering a movement for a wildlife sanctuary in South Park, but the League was successfully opposed by local ranchers; for the *Bayou Salado* was by then taken up completely with ranches.

Indians, explorers, trappers and hunters, miners, railroad builders, and ranchers—each entered the *Bayou Salado* in search of a promised land, and found it. First came the Indians to a bountiful hunting ground.

CHAPTER TWO

The Indian Hunting Ground

At the time that the first white people, the Spaniards, entered North America in the 1500's, the Ute Indians were well entrenched in the Central Rockies. The Utes roamed throughout the mountains of the area later known as Colorado. Their domain extended even into Utah, although the tribe numbered only about 10,000.

Who occupied these mountains prior to the Utes is unknown. The prehistoric migration of Asians over the Bering Strait occurred more than 20,000 years ago; but it is supposed that the Utes, a Shoshonean tribe, entered the Colorado Rockies only a thousand years ago. The Woodland Indians came to eastern Colorado at least by 400 A.D., probably from Nebraska. They occupied the lower foothills of the Front Range near the plains, but whether they entered the mountains and South Park is unknown; nor is it certain whether the Utes came into contact with them near the foothills and plains.

The short, dark-skinned Utes were related linguistically to tribes north, west, and south of Colorado. The tribe did no farming and had but the crudest weapons of stone. Their utensils were stone or basketware with almost no pottery. Blankets, sandals, and some clothing were woven from vegetable fibers, such as juniper and yucca, but also were made of skin.

The Utes depended so much on native plants and animals for their subsistence that it is not surprising that lush South Park was their favorite haven. Moving about in family groups, or small bands, the Utes gathered their food. The women collected seeds, wild currants, chokecherries, wild strawberries, raspberries, yucca pods, prickly pears, and insects in their large willow baskets. Many of the seeds were ground on flat stones, or metates, with a hand stone, or mano; the insects were roasted. The men hunted buffalo, elk, deer, bear, mountain sheep, antelope, rabbits, prairie dogs, squirrel, fish, ducks, quail, and wild turkeys—all to be found in South Park. Even eagles were hunted but probably for feathers rather than for food. Birds and rodents usually were snared or sometimes smoked out of burrows. Prior to hunting with horses, the Indians caught buffalo by surrounding one with a circle of men and then shooting it with arrows. The women prepared the hides by scraping away the flesh and hair with stone and bone implements and then stretching them and smoking them.

Despite the mobility which was to be achieved with horses, the Utes still had to store quantities of buffalo meat for the winter. They jerked it, slicing it thin and then drying it in the sun. They also made pemmican by pounding dried meat mixed with parched berries. The crushed mixture was put into skins over which melted fat and marrow were poured.

Arrowheads were flaked and chipped from jasper and quartz. Stone quarries of the Indians are found in many places in South Park, a notable one of quartz and agate being in the Antelope Springs area. Not only were the common, Western plains type of points made, but the Utes also fashioned larger ones, deeply lobed and notched. These were eight or more inches long; and, when used on the end of a pole, they must have been unusually effective cutting weapons with their barbed edges.

The only archeological study which has been done in South Park has been surface work. Large concentrations of finds of arrowheads are not at battlefields but at semi-permanent campsites where weapons were made and where game or bodies were brought in. Blades, scrapers, borers, knives, drills, awls, and points—including some Yuma and Folsom points — have been found. Two of the largest and finest collections, the Turner Collection and the Hand Collection, are now on display in the South

Park City Museum at Fairplay. Small animal effigies of stone, including the eagle, have been picked up in the park. No baskets have been found and only small bits of pottery. There are no pictographs or petroglyphs found in the area.

Forty-seven sites were located during an anthropological study made by the University of Denver in 1944. Manos, metates, and tipi rings were frequently discovered with the usual points and artifacts. The study indicated that most of the sites were small temporary camps—not large, permanent camps of the type which would be used in winter. Instead, the Indians seem to have come into the park to hunt during the summer and fall. Many of the small sites found on exposed hills and spurs were for signal stations or lookouts. Campsites often were at the bases of slopes, but some large locations were on hills which contained camps, workshops, lookouts, and signal fires at one site.

Eight sites were found between Kenosha Pass and Fairplay, with another having been reported near Alma by the residents of that area. The University researchers found a Folsom point at Red Hill. Such a discovery does not prove that Folsom Man was in South Park, however; it merely suggests that a later Indian might have picked up the point elsewhere and brought it to the park with his weapons.

The most numerous sites, sixteen in all, were between Fairplay and Antero Junction. In the southern half nearly every hill has a site. And along High Creek and the South Fork of the South Platte, the ridges had several camps. East of U.S. 285 near the turn-off to Weston Pass, a row of hills has an important site of several acres. Here there were a camp, a workshop, red stone quarries, a lookout, and many manos, metates, and Yuma points.

Near Salt Creek and the salt marshes in the area of today's Antero Reservoir, the Indians often camped. They came to the spot to get salt for their own use but, equally enticing, to hunt the game which grazed on the grasses where salt and water were also plentiful. Three sites were found on the southwest shore of Antero Reservoir. Here obsidian points and Rio Grande points have been picked up. Another important site was near the south shore of the reservoir, but its location is under water and can

23

be seen only when the lake level is low. This very old site included a camp, a workshop, a quarry of poor red quartzite, and a burial.

There was a total of ten sites from Trout Creek Pass to Hartsel. A little over five miles east of Antero Junction and about nine miles west of Hartsel, a very large campsite and a battleground were found near the base of Twin Peaks. Mrs. Thomas McQuaid, who lived most of her life at the Salt Works Ranch a few miles to the north, reported that there were excavations and fort-like constructions here. Around Hartsel, where the hot springs attracted the Indians, six sites were located.

Although only four sites were found betwen Hartsel and Fairplay along Colorado Route 9, perhaps the most interesting one in the park is in this section. One-half mile north of Garo a campsite occupied four acres on both sides of the road. The line of rocky outcroppings here provided a natural fort. There was a good spring just to the north as well as plenty of water in the valley along the Middle Fork of the South Platte. Around 1907 Frank Turner of Garo found an Indian burial on the ridge opposite the town. Usually the Utes either cremated their dead or buried them in rock crevices. However, this Indian had been placed beneath two rock slabs which had been propped up to effect a cave.

There were four sites in the southeastern area near Elevenmile Canyon Reservoir. In fact, one site is now an island in the reservoir. Although a large battle is supposed to have taken place in this vicinity, the study made no mention of a battleground here.

No attempt was made to date the sites. Being found on the surface, they undoubtedly belong to fairly recent times. However, the artifacts were confined to the primitive stone weapons of hunters and warriors.

After the Englishman George Frederick Ruxton visited Colorado in 1847 and 1848, he wrote of his travels in *Mexico and the Rocky Mountains* and *Life in the Far West,* and in them tells something about the Indians of South Park. During the trip he spent several of the winter months at a trader's fort where Pueblo now is located. From the trappers and traders who came there, he gathered his information about the mountains and the Indians.

Whether or not Ruxton actually visited some of the places which he described in his writing, and how reliable his sources were, become questions. For example, he wrote that *Bayou Salado* was a "favourite resort of the buffalo in the winter season, and also, for this reason, often frequented by the Yuta [Ute] Indians as their wintering ground." This statement is the source apparently of commonly held misunderstandings about the Utes' wintering in South Park.

When Thomas Jefferson Farnham passed through in 1839, he observed many campsites around the salt springs. He also said that buffalo came into the park "about the last days of July, from the arid plains of the Arkansas and the Platte; and thither the Eutaws [Utes] and Cheyennes from the mountains around Santa Fe, and the Shoshones or Snakes and Arrapahoes from the west, and the Blackfeet, Crows and Sioux from the north, have for ages met. . . . When their battles and hunts were interrupted by the chills and snows of November, they have separated for their several winter resorts." Although one might question Farnham's ethnology, his conjecture about seasonal migrations is probably correct.

Farnham continued that the Arapahoes hunted buffalo in the summer in the "New Park, or 'Bull Pen' " [North Park], in the "Old Park" [Middle Park], and in "Bayou Salade."

It is generally accepted that the Cheyennes and Arapahoes wintered on the eastern plains. They had first come into that area from the northeast, pushing the Comanches and Kiowas farther south. The Utes, on the other hand, remained in their original mountain domain but wintered primarily in the warmer valleys to the south or around Pagosa Springs.

The Utes had several trails in and out of the park, which served as a hub. Most of their trails used passes which have been occupied by roads in modern times. The principal ones from the east were Kenosha Pass leading in from the North Fork of the Platte and Wilkerson Pass from Ute Pass and the Pikes Peak country. To the south the Indians used Currant Creek Pass. However, they also had an important, but now forgotten, route from the southeast—the Oil Creek route which stemmed from the

25

Arkansas River a little east of Canon City and which came into South Park near Elevenmile Canyon Reservoir.

To the southwest a much-traveled trail led to the Salida area and Monarch and Poncha Passes into the distant valleys and mountains. This trail, now called the Ute Trail, was used often by bands crossing the park from Kenosha and Wilkerson Passes as part of one of the major Indian routes through the Rockies. In South Park the trail approximates Park County Route 53, or the Agate Creek road; but instead of running north of Cameron Mountain, as the present road does, it went down Badger Creek, passed south of Cameron Mountain, and then followed Ute Creek to the Arkansas.

Trout Creek Pass was a common route which provided access to the Arkansas River and the Elk Mountains. Weston and Mosquito Passes are also known to have been Indian trails into the Blue River country as were Breckenridge (Boreas), French, and Georgia Passes.

Farnham also mentioned in his account that he met Indians who spoke Spanish. The Utes were greatly affected by contact with the Spanish. By the 1600's the Indians were delivering to the Spaniards buffalo robes and deer hides, meat, and Indian hostages who became Spanish slaves. In return the Utes acquired horses, guns, metal, blankets, cloth, and assorted trinkets. Possessing horses, the Utes could travel much farther afield. Coming into contact with the Plains Indians, they took on some of the Plains culture. For instance, the Utes began to follow the buffalo onto the prairie, to live in large tipis which they could transport, and to trade for a little pottery. They also were able to band together in larger, more powerful groups.

However, just as the Utes were traveling onto the plains for buffalo on occasion, so too the Comanches and Kiowas, who had acquired horses in the 1700's, could enter the mountains for hunting. The Comanches, or Padoucas as they were called by the French, were at first friendly to the Utes; but rivalry over the hunting grounds soon broke out. Henceforth, the Utes fought one skirmish after another with the tribes of the plains; for South Park had become a hunting ground of the Comanche, Kiowa,

Cheyenne, and Arapaho. The Utes never relinquished their hold on the park, but neither did they achieve complete respite from enemy attacks before white settlement resolved the matter. The Comanches and Kiowas traveled into South Park off and on until the 1850's. The Cheyennes and Arapahoes began to appear in the park after 1815 and visited the area from time to time into the 1860's.

White travelers and settlers had opportunity to witness some of the brushes between the rival tribes. In June of 1843 when the second Frémont expedition passed through the park, they skirted an Indian battle near the site of Hartsel. The fight was between Arapahoes and Utes. Charles Preuss, the expedition's cartographer, noted in his diary, "A few howling women and fugitive horses were all we could see. It was most advisable for us to remain neutral. Therefore, we hurried past as fast as possible ... "

Kit Carson and two other trappers came into South Park for the winter beaver season in the fall of 1851. Since it was "too late" for Indians, they built a cabin and settled down to trapping. The next spring when Kit traveled to the south end of the park to get their horses, he witnessed a battle between the Comanches and Utes. According to the account of one of the trappers, William Drannan, the site was on a creek which ran due west from Pikes Peak and which afterward was called "Battle Creek." The location cannot be determined from this description. Perhaps the stream was the South Platte which does lie directly west of Pikes Peak in the southern end of the park but which flows easterly. On the other hand, both Twin Creek and West Fourmile Creek run westerly from the Peak, but they are outside South Park in the hills. At any rate, the contest had been arranged by the chiefs in the fall of the previous year. Carson found the Comanches' camp of brush wickiups set up on a hill near the south bank of the stream. The Utes had pitched camp on the opposite side. Observing all of the formalities of Indian warfare, the opponents spent two or three days hunting and preparing for battle. During this time the Comanches tried to recruit Carson into their forces; but the canny trapper, being uncertain as to which tribe would be victorious, elected to be a neutral observer. Drannan is not always a reliable source of facts on Carson, though.

Finally, amidst war whoops and the beating of tom-toms, the battle got under way. The weapons were arrows, tomahawks, and knives. For two days the fight progressed with the tribes charging and retreating. At supper time the fighting would cease, and no guards were needed at night. On the third day forty Utes were killed or scalped in a morning battle. In the afternoon the Comanches again charged the Utes, driving them back. When the Comanches returned to camp, they had a hundred Ute horses with them. That night the Utes left the battle site, temporarily dispossessed of their hunting ground.

Even after white settlement began, the warfare between the Utes and their rivals continued. In June of 1860 about 500 Indians of allied tribes pitched their tipis near the young town of Denver in preparation for an attack on the Utes in South Park. Despite the arrival of Jim Beckwourth and Kit Carson to persuade the allies to give up their plans, the war party moved on to South Park. Near the south edge of the park along the Platte, a camp of Utes was surprised. Several women and children were killed. However, the Utes succeeded in driving out the allies, who returned to Denver with four Ute boys as captives. Richard Whitsitt, a pioneer in Denver and Colorado City, adopted one of them.

A skirmish between Utes and Arapahoes occurred in the same year near Garo, the Utes being led by Colorow. This battle may have taken place as the Utes chased the allies back to Denver after the fight in June.

In July of 1861 a party of Arapahoes arrived in Denver from South Park. This band had in its possession eight Ute prisoners— five squaws and three babies—and six scalps. One squaw was forced to dance around the scalp of her husband, a chief who had been killed, while the other squaws were balefully mourning the murder of some of their infants. The prisoners also were submitted to other indignities which they accepted as the rule of Indian warfare. In a letter Newton Pettis, later an Associate Justice of the Colorado Supreme Court, described the episode as "wilder than a dream, and sadder than a death." He also protested that the local Indian agent might have resolved the affair merely by trading eight horses for the eight captives.

Government officials did intervene in behalf of the Utes on later occasions when the friendship of the tribe was being cultivated. In 1865 the Utes apparently suffered a loss of animals or goods at the hands of Mexicans somewhere within the Ute reservation to the southwest. John Evans, then the Territorial Governor and *ex officio* Superintendent of Indian Affairs, wrote to James Castello at Fairplay that he had given Chief Ouray and his Utes shirts and other goods and that he had promised them one or two thousand sheep. Evans instructed Castello to take to the Indians twenty sheep, two or three sacks of flour, and "a couple of beefs if you cannot get the sheep." Castello was also to assure Ouray—or "Colorado," as Evans called the chief—that "I am not for the Mexicans to do any harm to the Indians but will protect both, that I have ordered a great many sheep for them and will send him word to come and get them near the Salt Works when the goods come . . . " Hopefully, Evans kept his promise. Evidently he dealt fairly with the Indians, for in October of that year he was reported to have gone to South Park after delivering 7,000 sheep and other goods at Empire to some other Utes from Middle Park. This payment was part of an annual treaty obligation.

In 1868 the Indians created excitement among a party of Eastern dignitaries who were touring Colorado. The Colfax Party, about which more will be said in a later chapter, had just re-entered South Park from the west when they saw Indians circling nearby. The sophisticated politicos — including Vice-President Schuyler Colfax, Governor Bross of Illinois, and assorted friends, newspapermen, and female relatives—made a protective circle of their wagons in short order. 1868 was a year when the Plains Indians were making their last desperate raids and wars against the white men, so the group had reason to be even more nervous than dudes usually were. However, the Indians turned out to be about twenty-five friendly Utes who had been sent to escort the party back to Denver.

Having heard rumors in Denver that the Arapahoes were

headed for South Park, Frank Hall, Secretary of the Territory and Acting Governor, had rushed to the rescue of the party with the aid of the Utes. It is relevant, no doubt, that one of the young ladies in the Colfax Party was Hall's fiancée. She later laughed off the scare. She related that Colfax had announced his gallant plan to shoot the girls to save them from the Indians. But she claimed that he "didn't know one end of a gun from the other" and that she preferred to take her chances with the Indians. The party took on a carnival air as they rolled on down to Denver, accompanied by the braves dressed in handsome beaded buckskins and one Indian attired in a hand-me-down army coat with tails, a plug hat, and nothing else.

Of course, the white settlers developed a variety of strange notions about the "savages," one being that some of the chiefs and medicine men were Masons. The idea sounds like the product of a long winter in a lonely mining camp. In any event, a miner who was a Mason was reported to have been robbed by Indians on Boreas Pass. Remembering the legend about Masonic Indians, he gave the grand sign of distress. All of his goods were promptly returned, including a sack of flour which had been cut open. The bag was tied shut with what "competent judges" later declared to be authentic Ute Indian strings.

During the 1870's old Chief Colorow was the most familiar Indian in South Park. He and his companions annoyed the settlers by paying calls at houses where they demanded food and shelter. James Castello's earlier services to the Utes had made Colorow his friend, though. When Indians harassed the Castello family at their new store and hotel east of the park at Florissant, Colorow instructed Mrs. Castello, a petite but rugged little lady whom he called "Little Biscuit," to send smoke signals from a nearby hill to bring his assistance.

One night in 1880, following the Meeker massacre on the White River, most of the population of Alma fled down the valley to the courthouse at Fairplay to fort up against hordes of Utes who were supposed to be on the warpath. After much scurrying about and preparation for defense, it was revealed that a drunk miner had been enjoying a spree and had set off a false alarm.

30

Not long afterward, all of the Utes were removed to distant reservations, the Plains Indians having been sent off a dozen years earlier. The removal of the Utes ended about thirty years in which their land and rights in Colorado had been nibbled away. In 1849, after Indian raids on American supply trains headed for Santa Fe and the Mexican War, the Utes had been forced to accept the jurisdiction of the United States. All Ute territory was annexed to what was then New Mexico Territory. In 1863 the Utes ceded all of their domain except one large segment in Colorado on the Western Slope north to the Colorado and Roaring Fork Rivers. A treaty in 1868 defined the boundaries of this reservation within which the Utes were to have absolute rights, but these soon were violated by the whites. The Utes still were permitted to move about outside the reservation, and they frequently passed through South Park during this period on their way to an agency in Denver or to Colorado City and the springs at Manitou for a winter camp.

With the Ute removal in 1880 an era did not close, for it had already ended. The beautiful Indian hunting ground of *Bayou Salado* had been lost for more than a decade. The remnant of Utes who had wandered about South Park in decreasing numbers had been reduced successively to murderers, petty thieves, beggars, pests, and thorns in the consciences of the white possessors of their land. However, the Indians had managed to survive one era of whites—the explorers and the trappers.

31

CHAPTER THREE

The Ancient Quests in a New Land

Spaniards came into the Southwest seeking gold. Having conquered the Aztec and Inca empires in Mexico, the quest of more gold for Spain drew Coronado north in 1541 to what is now New Mexico. He also briefly penetrated the high plains of eastern Colorado and western Kansas, the region called *Quivera* by the Spaniards. It is known that during the 1600's Spaniards entered the San Luis Valley, where they hunted buffalo and opened up gold and silver mines. But on the whole, the mountain land north of New Mexico in the territory called *Teguayo* or *Tetago* remained unvisited, although a proposal was made in 1678 to explore it. Even when Hurtado traveled as far north as the junction of the South and North Platte Rivers in Nebraska in 1714 and 1715, he stayed east of the mountains.

By that time the French had reached the Central Rockies and soon visited South Park. The French had been pushing farther and farther west during the 1600's, never understanding how much more land lay beyond their outposts but expecting that sooner or later they would find Chinamen. (When Nicolet arrived at Green Bay in 1634, he had draped himself in a damask robe before stepping ashore to visit the "orientals" from the nearby wickiups.) Especially in the north, where New France authorized trading posts in the early 1700's, the traders were expected also to act as explorers to find the supposed waterway to the Northwest and the Orient.

For many, the first and the most unforgettable view of South Park is from the top of Wilkerson Pass, a route once used by the Indians.

This aerial view looking north toward Georgia Pass and the Park Range shows the northeastern section of South Park with the pre-Cambrian granite upthrust in the hilly, timbered area at the right. Mt. Evans is on the upper right. *U. S. Geological Survey, T. S. Lovering photo.*

On a hilltop near County Road 53, south of Hartsel, milky quartz was shattered by the Indians into chunks, from which arrow points and stone tools could be worked.

Sheep from the McDowell Ranch now graze within the natural stone fort where Ute Indians once fought battles with enemy bands of Indians from the plains. The present highway through Garo runs through the fort just north of town.

This view of Hamilton, the first mining town in South Park, is the only photograph know to exist of the town. Looking toward the northwest, the view is dominated by the Peabody Ranch, but a few of the old buildings of the town are on the left, though seen from the rear. Taken in the mid-1880's, the picture belonged to a Peabody daughter, Mrs. Frank Collard. *George White collection.*

A view from Windy Point looking southwest toward Como shows the tailings from the Fortune Placer covering the site of old Hamilton.

At the head of South Tarryall Gulch placers were worked in the earliest years of the gold rush and as late as the 1930's. These cabins were at a settlement called Little French Gulch, near Liebelt Junction and Deadwood.

Both of these views of Buckskin, or Laurette, were taken in 1864. The long ridge to the west of the town is Loveland Mountain. Just a corner of Mt. Bross is seen standing watch over the "liveliest little burg in South Park." *Upper photograph courtesy of the Library, State Historical Society of Colorado; and lower courtesy of the Denver Public Library Western Collection; both George D. Wakely photos.*

This old relic, which succumbed to vandalism in the 1930's, was thought to have been the original Park County Courthouse at Laurette (Buckskin). *Courtesy of the Library, State Historical Society of Colorado.*

Some of the old mines are again being worked as at this site in Buckskin Gulch. Snowy Mt. Cameron is seen beyond.

39

The foundations of a mill remain near Kite Lake at the head of Buckskin Creek above timberline, while the Kentucky Belle Mine which it served in the late 1800's was a thousand feet higher, at 12,500 feet.

An arrastra carved from a boulder on Buckskin Creek cups golden aspen leaves. A hundred years earlier, gold itself was separated from ore in this crusher just above the site of Buckskin.

40

When this arrastra was photographed on Mosquito Creek in the 1920's, the windlass was still intact. As the windlass turned, heavy stones rotated to grind up ores. *Carl Mathews photo.*

Father John L. Dyer, the "s n o w s h o e itinerant," cared for his scattered flock in the mining camps and ranches during the 1860's and 1870's, worked at placering when he was not out on his circuit, carried the mail during one lean winter on skis over the Mosquito Pass route, and recorded his hard, lonely adventures in *The S n o w - s h o e Itinerant. Courtesy of the Library, State Historical Society.*

The old stage station at Sterling in the Mosquito District, a mile west of Park City. The building dated back to the early 1860's for it was wall-papered with newsprint reporting the Civil War. *George White photo.*

A toll road was built across Mosquito Pass in the winter of 1878-1879 to provide a short, though harrowing, route to the booming town of Leadville. Four stagecoach and freight lines hauled the enormous traffic over the rough road which crossed the pass at 13,180 feet. *Courtesy of Tutt Library, Colorado College.*

This aerial view shows Mosquito Pass with the Sawatch Range beyond. The road at bottom passes the North London Mill and then climbs to the North London Mine. Note the aerial tramway between the mine and the mill, the first such tramway in Colorado. *U. S. Geological Survey, R. E. Landon photo.*

44

The North London Mill was served by a branch railroad in the 1880's and 1890's. The railroad was gone but the mill still operated in the 1930's. *Courtesy of the Denver Public Library Western Collection.*

North London Mine.

Deserted buildings of the North London Mine in 1964.

The South Extension of the London Mine with its large mill and a railroad spur became the center of operations, the major producer of the 1900's in South Park. A tunnel connected the North and South mines through London Hill. *Courtesy of the South Park City collection.*

Park City, west of Alma and near Sterling, or Mosquito, was a mining camp which sprang up in the late 1870's and which still has occupants. The Orphan Boy Mine, located here, has been worked intermittently for more than a century.

However, the main interest of the French farther south was in trapping. The area around the mouth of the Mississippi River had been claimed and settled in the late years of the 1600's as a commercial venture of France. The colony soon was sold to a private company that continued to promote trapping which had been initiated by the government. One report states that even before 1700 French trappers came up the Arkansas River to the vicinity of Pueblo, an event that roused the Spaniards to investigate. Etienne de Bourgmond is said to have seen Comanches in South Park in 1724. These occurrences predate the official French discovery of the Rockies in 1743 in Wyoming; therefore, the first Frenchmen in Colorado surely came from Louisiana rather than from the northern outposts of New France.

When in 1762 Louis XV ceded to Spain all of the French claims west of the Mississippi, to prevent these lands from falling into English possession, the only settlements were New Orleans and scattered trading posts. Many of the trappers and traders from these posts remained in the territory. It was because of their activity and because of the appearance of Americans on the fringes of the Spanish domain that the Spaniards finally decided to tighten up their control in the late 1700's.

Besides, the Spaniards were having a bad time with the Indians. When an official expedition from Santa Fe at last entered the heart of Colorado and South Park in 1779, the aim was to punish some of these offending Indians. In 1773 the Spaniards had chased Comanches into San Luis Valley to recover 200 head of horses, but the next year the Comanches merely increased their activity and made five devastating raids on Spanish settlers. When Juan Bautista de Anza became governor, he had a personal score to settle with the Comanches who had killed his father.

In August of 1779, de Anza himself led an army of 600 soldiers out of Santa Fe in search of Chief Cuerno Verde and his band. The Spaniards were joined before long by 200 Ute and Apache Indians who had their own losses to settle, having just been defeated by the Comanches at San Luis Lake. The force of 800 crossed Poncha Pass to the Arkansas River, which was forded near Salida. They then took the Ute Trail to the northeast into

South Park. Still pursuing the Comanches, the Spanish troops and the allies left the park past Pikes Peak. Later, down along Fountain Creek, a battle took place with several Comanches being killed, about sixty women and children captured, and 500 horses taken. However, Cuerno Verde escaped, so the chase continued to the Wet Mountains where he was killed on September 3.

A suit of Spanish armor is said to have been found in a rock crevice in the southwestern part of South Park. It probably belonged to one of de Anza's soldiers, for the expedition was the only recorded penetration of South Park by the Spaniards. The only other hints of Spanish activity in the park are unverified reports of Spanish mining of gold around the Buckskin area and an iron mine on the northwest slope of Mt. Silverheels. These legends seem doubtful, though.

After the victory in 1779 the Spaniards and Utes made a military and trade alliance. The Utes were to trade only with official Spanish agents, and the Spanish were to assist the Utes against enemy tribes. By the early 1800's the Utes were dissatisfied with the alliance, especially because the Plains Indians were gaining the advantage through trade with Americans. Then, after 1821 when Mexico became independent from Spain, the Utes' ally was gone. Much of the Ute and Spanish trade had been in the usual commodities, but another important item had been added—slaves. Apparently the taking of captives in many of the Indian skirmishes in South Park had a purpose other than war games. The slave trade was still being carried on between the Indians and Mexico in the mid-1850's.

1800 had marked a new era in the trans-Mississippi West, for Spain then lost a good portion of its land claims. Americans soon were to be moving into the West, including South Park, first intermittently in small numbers, then in a steady trickle, and finally in a great wave that swept everything on the land before it.

In 1800 Napoleon had forced Spain to return the lands to his new empire. But in 1803 the United States purchased the vast holdings. Following the Louisiana Purchase, Thomas Jefferson in 1806 sent Lieutenant Zebulon Montgomery Pike with a party of twenty-one men to explore the new possessions around the headwaters of the Platte. Whether Pike was also spying on the Spaniards for the United States Government or for Aaron Burr's traitorous designs is a much-debated question. In any event, the Pike expedition turned into either a hilarious comedy of errors or a grave miscarriage of responsibility.

Whatever Pike was supposed to be exploring, he seems to have been bent on one intention as his party followed the Arkansas toward the Rockies: he was tracking Spaniards to the Red River. While trading with the Pawnees in what is now Kansas, Pike discovered that a large force of Spanish cavalry had been at the Indian village, leaving flags furled there. Through the autumn Pike moved slowly toward the Rockies, following the trace of these Spaniards up the Arkansas. Arriving near the later site of Pueblo in November and hoping to gain a view of what lay ahead in the mountains, Pike and a few of his party spent several days in an unsuccessful assault on the Grand Peak (Pikes Peak) about fifty miles to the northwest. Lost in the mountains, the inadequately garbed men waded in knee-deep snow and finally gave up the venture. At any rate, the experience did forecast what lay ahead in the nature of misadventures.

The group then continued from Pueblo along the Arkansas into the mountains, still following the Spanish trace. On December 5 they camped at the site of Canon City. While some of the men spent four days in trying to relocate the elusive trace downstream, Pike and Robinson, the most able of Pike's men, explored the Royal Gorge. The expedition regrouped at Canon City after determining that the Spaniards had moved in that direction. On December 10 the American explorers marched "over the mountain" on an "excellent" road. Camping in a dry ravine, they killed a buffalo. The next day they marched one mile and then came to a Spanish campsite on a branch of the Arkansas. They followed this branch, with the trace appearing and disappearing every now and then, for two days and an estimated twenty-seven miles. On the third day, December 13, the party "passed large springs and the supposed Spanish camp and . . . a dividing ridge, and immediately fell on a small branch running N 20° W."

After a march north for about two miles, they came to a river

51

"forty yards wide, frozen over, which . . . ran northeast. This was the occasion of much surprise, as we were taught to expect to have met with the branches of the Red River, which should run southeast." Pike then conjectured that this river must be the headwaters of the Platte. The party had traveled about eighteen miles that day.

The river was the Platte, and Pike became the first official American explorer of South Park. It is generally agreed that Pike's route was up Oil Creek and into the park in the Elevenmile Canyon Reservoir area. This is the route described by Elliot Coues, an accepted authority on Pike. The other possible route, via Currant Creek Pass, is ruled out by the facts that Pike arrived at the Platte only two miles after entering the park and that there is no stream running northwest from Currant Creek Pass to the Platte. Instead, the small branch probably was Fourmile Creek. Furthermore, on December 14 the party moved up the Platte for four miles in a section where the "prairie" was only about two miles wide. This description, too, fits the terrain in the reservoir area.

Pike entered the following reports in his *Journal:*

[The prairie] was covered at least six miles, on the banks of the river, with horse dung and the marks of Indian camps, which had been [used] since the cold weather, as was evident by the fires which were in the center of the lodges. The sign made by their horses was astonishing, and would have taken a thousand horses some months. As it was impossible to say which course the Spaniards pursued, amongst this multiplicity of signs, we halted early and discovered that they or the savages had ascended the river. We determined to pursue them. As the geography of the country had turned out to be so different from our expectation, we were somewhat at a loss which course to pursue, unless we attempted to cross the snow-capped mountains to the southeast of us, which was almost impossible. [They already had proved impossible, for Pike was viewing the Pikes Peak massif again but from the other side!] . . . Killed two buffalo.

The entry for December 15 read as follows:

> After repairing our guns [three had "bursted"] we
> marched, but were obliged to leave another horse. As-
> cended the river, both sides of which were covered with
> old Indian camps, at which we found corn cobs. This
> induced us to believe that those savages, although er-
> ratic, must remain long enough in one position to culti-
> vate this grain, or to obtain it of the Spaniards. From
> their sign they must have been extremely numerous, and
> . . . possessed vast numbers of horses. My poor fellows
> suffered extremely with cold, being almost naked.

They camped again and on the next day they climbed an elevation, probably Spinney Mountain or Sulphur Mountain, and laid
out a route, abandoning the trace. They decided to leave the park
through the mountains to the southwest and, thus, to the "Red
River." In the meantime, one of the men had found a campsite
"which had been occupied by at least 3,000 Indians, with a large
cross in the middle. Query: Are those people Catholics?"

On December 17 the expedition came to the South Fork of
the South Platte and followed it for a few miles. But finding the
course to be too northerly, they struck off across the park. They
camped once more in the park and then crossed the mountains at
Trout Creek Pass.

After Pike left South Park, he did find a large river, which he
explored upstream. The party then followed it down river.
Imagine Pike's embarrassment when, after crossing hills to get
around a deep gorge, through which flowed the "Red River," he
found his Canon City campsite on the Arkansas at the other end
of the gorge.

The ill-starred expedition was next to have some harrowing
weeks crossing the snow-drifted Sangre de Cristo Range into the
San Luis Valley. Here Pike was picked up by the Spaniards,
whose territory he had entered when he left the Arkansas River.
He was taken as a prisoner to Santa Fe, where he busied himself
with the taking of notes. After his release he returned to the
States by way of Mexico and Texas.

While Pike was in Santa Fe, he had met an American trader who had been in South Park the previous year. Possibly this man, James Pursley, was the first American in the park; but there is too little recorded information about the earliest trappers and traders to be certain. The mountain men began to filter into Ute country in 1804. They hunted and trapped in South Park, the San Luis Valley, and the mountains around Taos, New Mexico; and they traded in Santa Fe and Taos. Pursley was one of the better known men of the fifteen or so Anglo-American trappers and traders who headquartered in Santa Fe in the early years of the business.

Pursley, originally from Kentucky, was in St. Louis in 1802. There he joined two other men who were leaving for the West to trap and to trade with the Osage Indians. The little group met a French *voyageur* on the Missouri and, consequently, wound up among the Mandan Indians. Pursley hunted and trapped for the Frenchman with "Paducas" and Kiowas until in the spring of 1805 Pursley and the Kiowas were driven by Sioux into the mountains.

The fleeing group camped in South Park. Pursley claimed that there were 2,000 Kiowas and 10,000 animals at their camp. He and two of the Indians went on to Santa Fe to determine whether the Spaniards would allow trade with them. Suitable arrangements were made, and Pursley remained in Santa Fe while the Indians returned to their band. In relating this story to Pike, Pursley also mentioned that he had found gold in South Park.

Although the printing of Pike's *Journal* in 1810 helped to introduce Easterners to the immense Western possessions, Lewis and Clark's expedition to the Northwest had already succeeded in attracting swarms of trappers into the sources of the Missouri River system. Many of the trappers began as employees of St. Louis fur companies but became independent when their contracts were up.

The trappers got their best beaver pelts in October and November when the furs were prime. The animals had glossy, thick winter coats by then, and the streams were still free of ice. The late plews, or prime furs, brought five or six dollars each sometimes and six or eight dollars at the peak of the trade.

The traps were set beneath the surface of the water and chained to a stick driven into the mud. A twig placed near the trap was sprinkled with strong musk from the castor glands of beaver as bait. After taking the drowned beaver from his trap, the mountain man skinned it, removing the oil sacks, and cut off the tail. The tail often was eaten. The boiled, gelatinous meat, which scarcely sounds appetizing at best, tended to be rather strong if the beaver had been feeding on willow, pioneer cookbooks report!

Although beaver abounded in the mountain valleys opening onto the *Bayou Salado,* the influx of trappers into South Park was slowed by the Spaniards and the Indians in the Southwest and the bordering lands of the Central Rockies. Only after New Mexico came under Mexican rule in 1821 did the activity in South Park begin in earnest. Other than Pursley, only one group of American mountain men, led by Ezekial Williams, is known to have been in the park prior to that date, although there probably were unrecorded expeditions.

Ruxton, repeating Fort Pueblo scuttlebutt of 1847, said that Williams first came to the park as early as 1800. Beyond that questionable report, it is know that Williams was in the *Bayou Salado* in 1813. He had been trapping since 1809 for the Missouri Fur Company around the headwaters of the Missouri. Late in the summer of 1812 he and nineteen men moved south to hunt around the Arkansas River. The next spring when Indians became troublesome, Williams' men moved into South Park. Here the party split up and left for other regions.

French *voyageurs* still worked the area for St. Louis companies, too. In the spring of 1826 James Pattie encountered a band of Utes who had just come from wiping out one of the less successful parties of French trappers in South Park. The Utes' plunder was six fresh scalps, five mules, an indefinite number of beaver skins, and dried buffalo meat.

Around 1826 mountain man Jim Beckwourth was in the park with a band of Crow Indians. Jim was a mulatto, but for all practical purposes he was one of the Crows, a chief in fact. He was the archetype of the mountain men—living with the Indians, living as the Indians, taking a squaw as his wife, and completely attuned to the harshness and the lonely beauty of the land. He and the Crows had succeeded in stealing 118 horses at the head of the Arkansas when they escaped with their stock into what, by description, must have been South Park. Here they found three more Indians with a small herd of horses. Shortly Jim and the Crows had two scalps and fourteen more horses.

The number of independent companies working the Rockies increased rapidly after the mid-1820's. One of these, the Bean-Sinclair party, crossed 10,000-foot Kenosha Pass into South Park in 1830. Many of the men in the large party were laid up with sickness in the park; so, when winter came, they moved on down to Santa Fe. Bill Williams with two other trappers is known to have been in the park also during 1830, having come in from Taos.

During the fall of the same year Kit Carson, who had come West in 1826, joined Thomas Fitzpatrick's party and spent the winter trapping in the mountains. The party was increased by the arrival of Blackwell with fifteen more trappers. The entire group moved camp from the upper Arkansas over into South Park near the Salt Springs, where the Indians tried to run off their horses. In the spring Carson with four others joined the Gantt party which also was in the park. Captain Gantt (or Gaunt) and Carson were old friends. They went on to North Park but returned to South Park the next spring after wintering on the Arkansas east of the mountains.

In the spring of 1833 Gantt was in the *Bayou Salado* again. Carson's party was on the Arkansas having a bad time of it. Two of his men left, taking with them 400 pounds of Carson's beaver skins. In the meantime, Indians repeatedly attempted to steal his horses. Finally Gantt sent four men over to help his friend. Carson, however, stuck with the trade and returned to the *Bayou Salado* often in later years.

The stream of trappers was steady throughout the 1830's, many of them for the Rocky Mountain Fur Company. There was "Colonel" Joseph Meek, who first came into the mountains with

William Sublette. In full military garb, Meek was leading his own party when he came into the park in 1834.

And Uncle Dick (Richens) Wootton trapped there in 1836. He had come out from Kentucky, arriving at Bent's Fort in eastern Colorado that year. During his season in *Bayou Salado* he gathered 1,000 pounds of skins which he was able to sell at seven dollars a pound. With that profit Uncle Dick bought up some goods and became an Indian trader—a career which lasted for a quarter of a century.

Bent's Fort on the Arkansas River was the first permanent trading post in Colordo. It was built in 1833 by Charles and William Bent and Ceran St. Vrain. Furs from South Park were taken down the Arkansas to the Fort. There was no rendezvous point, like Brown's Hole to the northwest, for the trappers in the mountains around South Park. For the most part until the building of Bent's Fort, furs were cached until being taken to Taos and Santa Fe or directly to St. Louis. However, in 1832 Gantt and Blackwell had built a trading post about six miles from the present site of Pueblo. This post was gone by 1835. Another post was built in 1839 a few miles west of Bent's Fort. It was called El Pueblo or Peeble's Fort. Then in 1842 some of the mountain men, including Jim Beckwourth, went together to build a fort and trading post at Pueblo to serve the trappers who used the Arkansas River.

But by 1845, with silk replacing fur in hats and with the usual vicissitudes of fashion in coats, beaver skins were not in demand and had dropped to only a dollar or even less per pound. The beaver were not gone, but the trappers were out of business. They could not meet the cost even of equipment at that price.

Not all of the mountain men left, however. There were men like John Smith who stayed. Smith had been trapping the mountains for ten years when he took up with a band of Cheyennes in South Park. He also took up a squaw, complete with a lodge and horses. He hunted buffalo and became a trader in robes. Much of the robes and meat that he dressed went to New Mexicans who brought pumpkin and corn to trade. When the gold-seekers came in 1858, they found Smith and his squaw trading with Cheyennes at the site of Denver. He was one of the organizers of the Denver City Town Company, and obligingly lent out one half of his cabin for the first Episcopal Church service in Denver and the other half for gambling. Smith was with the Cheyennes when the Americans attacked the Indians at Sand Creek.

In the 1840's expeditions into the West for pleasure trips and for exploration began to appear in increasing numbers. These men were pursuing what they called America's Manifest Destiny. In other words, they were bent upon securing, opening up, and exploiting the Western territory. Usually the expeditions were guided across the wilderness by the mountain men, just as Kit Carson worked for Frémont in 1842, 1843, and 1844.

The first of the sight-seeing expeditions was that of the aforementioned Thomas Jefferson Farnham of Peoria, a lawyer whose manifest destiny seems to have been merely to get away from home long enough to see the West and the Hawaiian Islands. He then returned to Peoria and wrote about his grand adventure. However, Farnham was both observant and as factual as possible in his accounts, and his writing whetted the desire of other Americans to see the sights for themselves.

With a party of sixteen and a guide named Kelly, a trapper who had been in the West for a dozen years, Farnham crossed South Park in the spring of 1839 en route to Oregon. Their route into the park followed Oil Creek. The party saw several bull buffalo in the park, but the animals were so poor that the men made no effort to shoot them. Fresh hoof marks of horses dragging lodge poles were crossed, so Kelly, predicting that the "Eutaws" would drive off the buffalo to prevent the Americans' laying up any meat, decided that they should shoot the next buffalo that they found. After getting one, they moved on across either Hoosier or Boreas Pass and so down the Blue River country.

In December of 1842 Rufus B. Sage was returning to the East from Oregon when snow forced him to take a more southerly route through Middle Park and South Park. Sage entered the *"Bayou Salâde"* via Hoosier Pass, "over the dividing ridge by a well-beaten buffalo trail, to the right of Long's Peak [*sic*]." After camping for a few days, the party moved on across the park on a trail well-marked by buffalo. However, the "horses frequently became so mired in snow we were compelled to extricate them by main strength . . . " In addition, magpies troubled the mules by pecking at their sore backs until these were covered with buffalo hides. Game, including the buffalo, was abundant. Sage's travels later appeared in print under the enticing title *Rocky Mountain Life; or Startling Scenes and Perilous Adventures in the Far West, During an Expedition of Three Years.*

Bent on more practical purposes, Frémont's second expedition came through the park twice in the following year, 1843. Lieutenant John C. Frémont of the Corps of Topographical Engineers had made an exploration through the West in 1842 in an effort to find a short route to the Northwest. In 1843 he again set out, this time to extend his surveys down the coast of California. The group made several detours on its way West before the party had secured adequate personnel and supplies. On one of these detours Kit Carson was employed at Pueblo as guide, an assignment that he had also filled in 1842. Some of the men proceeded to St. Vrain's Fort from Pueblo by way of the springs at Manitou and Ute Pass, South Park, and North Park.

On the return trip in June the expedition again came through the chain of parks—North, Middle, and South. They entered South Park over Hoosier Pass on June 22. There the expedition's phlegmatic cartographer, Charles Preuss, became a little more cheerful than usual when he realized that, after Hoosier Pass, the trip should be downhill all the way. However, the group had to skirt a Ute-Arapaho battle (see Chapter II) and then scramble about in the hills around Oil Creek, much to Preuss's disgust, before they were out of the park and on their way home, downhill all the way.

Returning from California in 1844, Frémont again came through South Park over the well-established Hoosier Pass route, with Carson once more as guide. On this occasion as the explorers were entering the park, Arapahoes had solicited aid in fighting a band of Utes. The whites declined. The next morning the Arapahoes raided the Ute camp. Then the Utes came soliciting the white men's aid. Again the Frémont party declined. This time, with the Indian fight crackling nearby, the white men forted up about fifteen miles away. In the expedition's accounts there is nothing to indicate that the party was engaged in the fighting. However, at the Shattinger Ranch on Michigan Creek, about six miles northwest of Jefferson, there are mounds which are reputed to be Frémont's fort. Old canteens, buttons, and guns are said to have been found there. Leaving the park, Frémont dropped straight south to Currant Creek Pass, the Guffey area, West Fourmile Creek, and Oil Creek.

According to Ruxton's accounts, a half-breed Pueblo Indian named "Mattias" and Parson Bill Williams guided him into South Park late in the winter of 1847-48. Ruxton told of his pleasures as a solitary camper and hunter there. Back in England Ruxton yearned for this idyl, and he died in 1849 during a second trip to America on his way to the Far West. He had hoped to follow the Arkansas to *Bayou Salade* where he would winter before moving on to the Pacific Coast.

Nor could Kit Carson quite bring himself to leave South Park and the old days of the mountain man forever. It was as late as 1851 and 1852 when, according to yarn spinner William Drannan, Carson trapped in the park with him. Frank Hall's *History of Colorado* says that John Albert trapped near Hamilton in 1851, so perhaps Albert was with Carson. The party built a cabin that same winter in the valley of Tarryall Creek. Here the gold towns Tarryall and Hamilton were to spring up in less than a decade. Albert later reminisced that there was plenty of beaver "but no gold in paying quantities."

In the early summer of 1852 Carson went on to Middle Park and the Laramie River. He came again through the *Bayou Salado* as he headed back to Taos. Then the mountain man left the park for the last time. He must have looked back at the shimmering valley and the crystalline peaks with nostalgia for an era gone forever.

What was this strange allure of South Park? It was more than just game and robes to trade, furs and dollars over the counter at a down-river post, land to add to an empire and a way to get to someplace else. It was adventure and solitude, a place to test a man, and a place to make peace with life, a place to forget what had gone before and a place to begin again. It was an unspoiled land, the dream.

CHAPTER FOUR

Mining: 1859-1860

The Spanish quest for gold in North America was long forgotten, the French and American fur trappers were gone, and
for a few short years the Indians were once again in sole possession
of the *Bayou Salado*. But in 1858 a motley group of Cherokee
Indians and white Georgians, organized by Green Russell, were
poking about in the stream beds of the park. Although they found
some gold, it was not in interesting quantities.

They were not surprised to find gold in the park. Pursley in
1806 had reported it was there. Also, a French *voyageur* named
Du Chet had shown people in Santa Fe a pouchful of nuggets
which he had picked up in South Park in the 1830's. When the
New Mexicans hired him to guide them to the spot, though, he
could not find it again. Parson Bill Williams had found a few
nuggets while he was trapping in the *Bayou Salado* in the fall of
1848. And Colonel William Gilpin, a promoter who later was the
first governor of Colorado Territory, reported that he had found
gold at Cherry Creek, Clear Creek, the Cache la Poudre River,
Pikes Peak, and South Park while he was leading troops against
hostile Indians during the Mexican War.

The discoveries, though, were paltry as compared with what
was happening in the California gold fields, so they were largely
ignored until the financial panic of 1857 prompted a host of bank-
rupt Easterners to go to the Rockies looking for means to get
back on their feet. The first prospectors of 1858 were followed

by a swarm in 1859 when word got out that good placers had been found at Cherry Creek and Chicago Creek. With the Gregory Gulch discovery (at Central City) in May, the rush was on.

In June of 1859 a group of prospectors, including J. B. Kennedy, Dr. J. L. Shank, and D. M. Slaughter, came over the mountains from the Gregory Diggings to South Park. Here the group was attacked by Indians but escaped with all scalps intact. On July 9 the party again was set upon, and this time Kennedy, Shank, and five or six others were killed at what is called Deadman's Gulch near Kenosha Pass.

When word of the murders reached Gregory Diggings, a party set out to catch the guilty Indians. Not finding the culprits, the posse risked stopping to prospect for a while, and another group joined them. During July, with the Indians continuing to harass the white intruders, the newcomers killed several Indians.

In the first group which arrived in July were Earl Hamilton, William J. Holman, and five others. (Hamilton and Holman founded the rival towns of Hamilton and Tarryall in 1860.) The second group included six men either from Wisconsin or from the Wisconsin Mining District near Gregory (or both). After pausing to survey the breath-taking view above South Park, they named the pass in the northeast corner of the park, over which they entered the valley, Kenosha Hill or Kenosha Summit.

The men went up Tarryall Creek north of the present town of Como and found there the old log cabins of John Albert and other trappers. Thinking that prospects looked good there, they lingered and found exciting pannings. This strike on the Tarryall, which brought hundreds of prospectors thronging into the area in two weeks, was made about four miles above Como, near the forks of Tarryall Creek and Deadwood Gulch. The original discoverers staked out fourteen 100-foot claims along the stream. However, a site two miles downstream seemed to provide a better location for a settlement, and here activity centered where the open land to the south meets the mountain valley to the north. (The present town of Tarryall, at a different location in the Tarryall Mountains, came into existence in 1896 and was at first called Puma City.)

As the crowd of prospectors arrived, some of them explored the surrounding land. On Beaver Creek, rumor said, Daniel Pound had found scales of gold as big as watermelon seeds and worth twenty-five cents or more than a dollar each. In all of the excitement, prospectors thought that "Pound's Diggings" meant a pound-a-day in yield, and more prospectors flocked in.

By August all of the Tarryall Diggings was staked out, and the claim owners were refusing to subdivide their locations with disappointed late comers. The latter dubbed the diggings "Graball" with a note of spleen. However, the land around the junction of Beaver Creek and the Platte River looked good, and here gold was discovered on August 19. The prospectors, glancing over their chipped shoulders toward "Graball," named the new location "Fair Play."

All of these first mining claims were placers, where gold had been deposited in the gravel and sand along the stream beds and was found by panning. Erosion had already done much of the job of separating the gold from rock, but nature also had separated the gold in the placers from its original lodes somewhere farther back in the mountains. Therefore, a prospector always hoped that he might find another pocket or even the original vein.

At Buckskin Joe, about eight miles northwest of "Fair Play" and about two miles west of present-day Alma, one such lode was discovered in September of 1859. (A lode is a very large vein or a location in which several veins run close together.) The Buckskin Diggings had opened up as a placer when mountain man Joseph Higganbottom (or Higginbottom) led five prospectors up a gulch branching off the Middle Fork of the South Platte. The placers located by the party were on a stream then called Fairchild's Branch, named for one member of the group, but later called Buckskin Creek. Joseph Higganbottom was a mulatto trapper whose frontier garb had earned him the nickname "Buckskin." On August 19 the district was officially named in his honor.

A month later a man called Phillips came into the gulch and located a rich claim which was known as the Phillips Lode. Although the name itself indicates that he knew that his strike was something rather special, Phillips left the claim shortly and disappeared. The rich yield of the lode remained undeveloped until 1860.

Late in 1859 John H. Smith, Cornelius Griswold, Willis Bryant, and George W. Lechner also opened up the "Snow Blind District of Gilpin Gulch" at the foot of Hoosier Pass. This location was later to become Montgomery.

Then, with winter coming, all but about 150 of the prospectors at the Tarryall Diggings returned East or to Denver, Colorado City, or Canon City. The remaining miners settled down for as congenial a winter as possible. H. Z. Solomon, for instance, reported to the *Rocky Mountain News* that the citizens of "Tarry All" had met at the store of Wing, Doyle and Company on November 22, 1859, for the purpose of organizing the Tarry All Lyceum, a debating society. The Lyceum provided many an evening's rousing entertainment in the Diggings as long as the settlement existed. (When summer returned, Solomon was to be found engaged in the freighting business with George Wing, hauling goods into the Blue River district by way of Georgia Pass.)

The winter's lull in mining activity was merely a time of preparation for the big rush, not only by the prospectors but also by the town companies, road companies, freight companies, and merchants who were busy getting organized at the base of the mountains. The problem of getting to the placers was not easily solved. Although Denver City was the only supply town early in 1859, prospectors could not reach South Park from Denver except by foot on the Indian trail over Kenosha Pass. The interlocking hogbacks and foothills southwest of Denver presented a maze that defied any quick answer.

Consequently, some Denver men went south in August of 1859 to locate a supply town, Colorado City, on Fountain Creek near the later site of Colorado Springs. From this town prospectors traveled up Ute Pass and around behind Pikes Peak to reach Tarryall Creek near Lake George. They then followed that stream northwest between the Puma Hills and the Tarryall Mountains, across the northern end of South Park, and so to the diggings. However, the steepness of the old Indian trail near the foot of Ute Pass posed a problem to wagons, and with the exception of a half-dozen sturdy rigs, travel was on foot or horseback.

As a result, still another supply town sprang up in October, 1859, at Canon City. The route up the Arkansas past the new town and over the easy ascent of Currant Creek Pass, which reached only about 9500 feet in altitude, was favorably received, although prospectors coming to the Rockies from the East by way of the Arkansas found it far more useful than did travelers from the northeast, for whom the route was too roundabout. The first settlers at Canon City immediately began to lay out a road to Tarryall eighty miles away on a trail long used by Indians and trappers coming up from Taos or the Arkansas River by way of Currant Creek. The road was finished early in 1860 with some relocating, the entire length being marked with mileposts. The town of Canon City also was to provide a roisterous winter head-quarters for prospectors in the following three years, but it was nearly deserted when mining fell off in 1864.

In the meantime, the Colorado City Town Company had de-cided to improve the trail up Ute Pass. George Bute, one of the town founders, managed to get an ox team and wagon to South Park in January, 1860, over the route, although the trip took so long that he ran out of supplies by the time that he got to Floris-sant and had to go back for more. When H. A. W. Tabor and his wife took a wagon over the pass to South Park and California Gulch in February, the road still was scarcely begun. Tabor and the two men with him even worked on the road construction for a few weeks. When they started across with the wagon, the as-cent was so difficult that Augusta Tabor said they could see the smoke from the previous night's campfire at the end of each day. They hacked their way for a month, making their own road as they went, before they covered the fifty miles to Wilkerson Pass and saw South Park lying before them. The Ute Pass road was not finished until summer when, being a free road, it was heavily traveled.

Tabor, the future silver king of Colorado, camped for a few days with his little group on the Platte in South Park when they finally reached it. They went fishing and spent their evenings playing whist around their campfire. When the men went hunting, they got lost and Augusta had to guide them into camp with a signal fire. Although they tried to locate the route to the Arkansas by using Frémont's maps and letters, they finally gave up and followed their own hunches to Trout Creek Pass. Their last campsite in the park was at Salt Creek. There a prospector's stray burro wandered into camp on a cold night and stood in the hot ashes of the campfire, burning his fetlocks. The burro stayed with the Tabors and carried Augusta to California Gulch.

The provisional Legislature of Jefferson Territory, an unconstitutional body which Coloradans organized to provide some immediate authority, proposed a road to South Park from Denver in November of 1859. In December it authorized the organization of the Apex and Gregory Road; the Denver, Auraria and South Park Wagon Road; and the Golden City, St. Vrain, and Colorado Wagon Road—all to South Park.

The first of these roads built to the park was the Apex and Gregory Road, a toll road constructed in the winter of 1859-60. The first part of the route was on the original road to Blackhawk and Central City. Apex was in Mount Vernon Canyon west of Denver. A road by way of Bergen Park connected the Apex and Gregory Road with the North Platte Canyon route to Kenosha Pass.

The Denver, Auraria, and South Park Road left Denver to the south, and crossed the South Platte at Piedmont over a toll bridge, eight miles south of Auraria. The legislature authorized tolls of twenty-five cents for a wagon and team, ten cents for a horse, and five cents for each head of cattle. Having proposed the tolls and the route for the first eight miles, the legislators then pointed toward the tangled knot of foothills to the west and said that the road should be "by the nearest route."

The road was chartered by Robert B. Bradford, the uncle of William Bradford Waddell who helped to organize the Pony Express. In 1859 Bradford, Waddell, William H. Russell, and

Alexander Majors opened a freighting business in Denver, and Waddell and Majors also inaugurated the Central Overland California and Pikes Peak Express Company. Bradford came to Denver in the fall of 1859. In January of 1860 he laid out the town of Bradford City about fifteen miles southwest of Denver, and on the surrounding land he grazed the stageline's cattle. The ranch and town were behind the hogbacks south of Morrison and Colorow's Cave.

By mid-January a road of some sort was in existence passing through the hogbacks at Dutch Creek Gap. In February the Bradford Wagon Road Company had nearly finished building Brown's Bridge across the Platte south of Denver. However, by July, which should have been the peak of the traffic to the gold fields, all that existed at Bradford City was about thirty already vacant houses. Perhaps the occupants had taken the road to the mines themselves. The road left the empty town site and climbed an extremely steep hill. Half way up was a toll gate with a charge of $1.50. The road then crossed over the hill to Conifer, which was called Bradford Junction, and on to Kenosha Hill. Although the Bradford Road Company was bankrupt by the end of the year, probably because of the difficult hill ascent and the equally steep tolls which discouraged travelers, the road was used some through the 1860's until the Turkey Creek route was finished in 1867.

The third of the roads was begun in December, 1859, and was finished in April. This free road, which was used heavily, was the Golden City, St. Vrain and Colorado Wagon Road, running from Fort St. Vrain to Golden, Bergen Park, and South Park. South of Bergen Park this road joined the Bradford Road at Bradford Junction.

However, the practice of prospectors who were traveling light seemed to be to cut through the hogbacks by way of the handiest canyon—especially Bear Creek or Turkey Creek—and so over the hills to the Platte Canyon.

Once over Kenosha Hill into the park, some of the prospectors continued on to Breckenridge by way of Georgia Pass or by way of the Tarryall Diggings and Tarryall Pass (or Hamilton, Breckenridge, or Boreas Pass as it was successively called). Occasionally travelers to Breckenridge went by way of "Fair Play" and Hoosier Pass, which was named by some unknown prospector from Indiana.

Whichever road the travelers took to the gold fields, the lanes were well marked with abandoned wagons and broken parts. One prospector wrote home that blacksmithing was bound to be a better business than mining.

Prospectors were advised to bring plenty of food, especially sour, dried fruit and vinegar to prevent scurvy. For some whim of taste, the goldseekers also considered canned oysters an essential part of the diet. When the oysters were finished, the cans went into service as containers for gold nuggets or dust.

William Hedges and three other men equipped themselves for a trip to South Park with a typical outfit and provisions. They had a wagon with three yoke of oxen, a tent, tools—including picks, shovels, and gold pans—a wooden bucket, a dutch oven and kettles, tin plates and cups, flour, bacon, dried beef, lard, beans, dried fruit, coffee, pickles, three gallons of brandy, soap, gunpower, lead, shot, gun caps, ten yards of drilling for a sluice, candles, rope, a five-gallon water keg, and so on *ad infinitum*— all for a little over $600, or $158.58 per man.

As the snow disappeared in the spring of 1860, the wave of prospectors rushed in. At the Tarryall Diggings two towns sprang up. In June, William Holman laid out the town of Tarryall, a cluster of tents and cabins at the second location of the diggings. The other town, Hamilton, was located across the creek from Tarryall and upstream about a half-mile. Since Tarryall was on the far side, the south side, of the stream, that town attempted to compete with Hamilton later by building a free bridge as well as a road to the mines to lure travelers across the creek.

Hamilton, which was laid out by Earl Hamilton, and Tarryall were constantly vying with one another for development and prestige. Since the whole section often was referred to simply as "Tarryall," it becomes impossible at times to distinguish what was going on in which town. However, it seems safe to assume that Tarryall City was little more than a "residential suburb" of

Hamilton. As late as August in 1860, one still had to get to Tarryall City by crossing the stream on a ten-foot pole.

Hamilton, on the other hand, rapidly became the center of activity for the entire district in the north end of the park. The town was built on one main street between the creek and the wooded hillside. The rutted street was usually crowded with oxen. By late June there were about forty houses while the remainder of the three thousand emigrants who had rushed into the district were camping in tents around the town and through the valley.

The Southern Stage Company had built large stables, and Hinckley and Company Freighters opened an office. St. Vrain and Easterday had a wholesale provision store. In addition, there were ten retail stores, three boardinghouses and a hotel, several saloons, two blacksmiths and five stock ranches, a recorder, and a justice of the peace.

The amount of business carried on was not so enormous as might be supposed. Most of the prospectors tried to economize by bringing enough supplies to tide themselves over for the summer until they returned home in the autumn. Furthermore, it would have been impossible for suppliers to provide all of the necessary provisions for the summer influx, anyway, in a territory which was still scarcely more than a wilderness.

In 1858, for instance, there was only one grist mill in the entire region—at Guadalupe in the southern part of present Colorado. By 1859 there was one at Huerfano (south of Pueblo) and another at San Luis. The latter was built by H. E. Easterday, who advertised in the *Rocky Mountain News* in April, 1860, that he had "a large and beautiful supply of American Mill Flour made at our mill in New Mexico" on hand at "Canon City, near Tarryall." Easterday was the same man who soon had a wholesale business in Hamilton. A fourth mill was built in 1860 in Fremont County. But these mills could grind only about six bushels of wheat a day—hardly enough to supply all of the goldseekers as well as the new settlers in the towns outside the mountains.

At Hamilton flour was selling for about twenty dollars a sack and coffee for five dollars a pound. No wonder that prospectors brought all of the provisions that they could from the East! However, beef cost only seven cents a pound—just about what it was worth since most of it was worn-out wagon stock. Trout, deer, and elk were plentiful, though.

All of Hamilton's first buildings were of log, for there was no sawmill. Hand-whipped native lumber cost $150 to $250 per thousand feet. Most of this sawed lumber was used in constructing sluice boxes.

Sluicing of gold replaced panning for the most part by 1860, but the principle involved in separating the gold from gravel was still simply a process of gravity. A sluice might be as long as 100 feet and about a foot and a half wide. Water was diverted through the sluice, into which gravel and sand were shoveled. Battens nailed on the bottom of the sluice caught the gold.

An effort was made to interject some religion into the bustle of mining activity when the Reverend William Howbert arrived toward the end of June to take charge of a new Methodist mission in South Park. He conducted the first church service on July 3 in Hamilton. The congregation pledged $200 for a church building, for which a lot was selected the next day. A contract for a building to cost $450 was let. However, by August, with the log church only two-thirds done, enough of the subscribers had drifted away that the construction never was finished. (During the summer Howbert traveled a circuit of the mining camps in the park. He and his young son Irving, who had accompanied him to South Park, left for Colorado City in August by way of the Tarryall Creek route. At that time, Howbert reported, there were no residents between the mines and Colorado City.)

In the meantime, Tarryall City had grown to a population of about 150 people late in July. And Messrs. Shields and Shakespeare built a new hotel, the Massasoit, which was unveiled with a grand ball for which Mrs. Shakespeare constructed a magnificent cake, worthy of newspaper coverage.

On July 26 a post office was established at Hamilton with Daniel Witter as postmaster. Hinckley and Company delivered the mail to the camps around Tarryall. The names of up to 20,000 miners were said to be recorded in the books of Hamilton's post office. Of these, 356 were named Smith, according to William Hedges. Hedges advised that anyone trying to reach a Smith by mail should be quite specific about the addressee—as, for example, "Cross-Eyed John Smith, William Smith the father of 12 grandchildren from Pike County, Illinois, or James Smith who failed in Keokuk, Iowa, in '57, for $60,000."

An enormous tent was set up in Hamilton with twenty gambling tables and a fiddler who, rumor said, was paid $100 a night to play out in front of the tent and draw in the crowds. Hedges, who had packed a flute somewhere in his bulging wagon, claimed that he was offered as much as the fiddler to play at the tent. However, Hedges spurned the crowds and the riotous night life to sit in front of his own sylvan shanty, where he played for his neighbors who lounged on the surrounding rocks.

For there was another side of the story of the gold rush—the side that told of the ninety-nine per cent of the lonely prospectors who did not make a strike. Hedges' story was one of these. When he first arrived, he moved into a recently deserted cabin with a dirt floor and roof. Before he had unpacked his wagon, though, a timber fire which he had casually noticed on the hill above town, moved down the slope and burned the cabin to the ground; so he set up his tent.

Next, he staked a claim on a bench of land to which water had to be diverted. Being an engineer and surveyor, he built a ditch with shares sold to other prospectors on the bench. Most of them failed to pay for their shares. No gold was found, anyway, and soon the bench was abandoned.

Claims farther up the gulch were paying up to $18 an ounce, so Hedges bought a claim there with a twelve-by-fourteen cabin on it. Most of the claims in the diggings were 150 or 200 feet long and there was a problem in getting enough water to run sluices on each claim, for those in the upper part of the gulch were able to divert it first. In September Hedges gave up, selling his claim for $50. Still not having enough money for stage fare home, he hired out to travel as helper with a family which was returning East.

Also, there was the fringe element which survived like pack

rats by snatching the product of other men's labor. One such fellow was a McFarland who had been tried at Empire for selling goods which he and a crony had stolen at Blackhawk. His punishment for that offense was thirty lashes and banishment from the diggings with half of his head shaved. McFarland next went to Tarryall Diggings where he was found robbing sluice boxes. The people of Tarryall, taking the direct approach to justice, hanged him.

Law was an impromptu business at best in the new mining districts. Not only were the Rockies far removed from any seat of government and authority, but the neighboring diggings in the mountains were also in different territories. Tarryall and all of South Park were in Kansas Territory, but Breckenridge and the Blue River on the other side of the Snowy Range divide were in Utah. Central City was in Nebraska Territory, and the San Luis Valley to the south was in New Mexico. It was far simpler for the settlers and miners to take the law into their own hands than to seek out the appropriate one of the four distant governments and to await its pronouncements.

The procedures for handling mining disputes were based on laws which the Gilpin miners had devised. Sometimes, as at Buckskin Joe, the laws adopted were merely a conglomeration of vagaries, however. So as to create some order and to settle conflicting claims, a miners' convention was called for September 22, 1860, at Hamilton. The delegates from the neighboring districts met at the St. Vrain Hotel there. A central government of the mining districts was organized, to be called the United Mining District. This district was divided into three sections: the Arkansas District, the Blue District, and the Park District. Albert E. Mathews, elected recorder of the Park District, was later a Park County lawyer and correspondent for the *Rocky Mountain News*. T. C. Wetmore was the president of the United Mining District, and W. J. Holman was the circuit judge. The District was to have four locations for holding court.

The Park District mines all were in the north end of South Park. In 1860 there were mines lining the banks of both Tarryall Creek and Deadwood Gulch, running back into the valleys be-

73

tween Mount Silverheels and Boreas Mountain. Also, mining was active on Georgia Pass, but these workings seem to have been on the north side of the ridge into the Blue River district, where buildings and mines are found today. The *Rocky Mountain News* in October, 1860, reported that $30,000 to $50,000 worth of gold was being taken out of Georgia Gulch weekly. Considerable activity took place in French Gulch, also, just over the ridge into the Blue District. The road to these gulches went up Michigan Creek from South Park and crossed Georgia Pass at 11,598 feet above sea level. A jeep trail still reaches this pass on the Continental Divide.

Jefferson City, or Jefferson Diggings, came into existence in 1860 near the foot of Georgia Pass, six miles northeast of Tarryall. The *Rocky Mountain News* in January of 1861 described Jefferson City's location as being "at the base of the mountain as you ascend to Georgia Gulch." About two thousand prospectors are said to have worked the area at Jefferson City.

This town was the only one in South Park shown on some of the earliest maps of 1860 and 1861. How long the camp lasted is not known, but it was deserted by 1864. In 1865 two new towns, Palestine and Jefferson, were proposed as a real estate venture. The two soon combined as Jefferson. It was laid out with lots sixty by one hundred feet in size, and it was promoted as a commercial and distribution center. Ten buyers from Hamilton and the same number from Georgia Gulch bought lots, agreeing to build. However, this town too was to be abandoned before the present Jefferson grew up at the same location as the Palestine-Jefferson venture, a few miles southeast of the original Jefferson City, in 1879.

About twelve miles below Hamilton several prospectors worked placers at Nelson's Bar in 1860. Nelson's Bar was four miles below the junction of Tarryall and Michigan Creeks. Although the miners found respectable quantities of gold and silver there, the workings never developed to any great extent.

Silver ores which reportedly were being sent from South Park to England for assay in October of 1860 may have come from Nelson's Bar; but, far more likely, they were obtained in the

Buckskin Joe and Hoosier Pass areas, or even around Tarryall where silver continually appeared in the gold sluices.

During 1860 Buckskin Joe had blossomed into the "liveliest little burg in South Park." "Buckskin Joe" Higganbottom had taken possession of and had begun to work the Phillips Lode, claiming also its excellent water rights. However, he soon traded the workings for a gun and a horse, gave up the water rights to pay off his whiskey bill, and left for the San Juan mines.

Jacob B. Stansell, Griff Harris, Miles Dodge, and J. W. Hibbard took over Higganbottom's claims. They laid out a town at a central point in the district, which was ten miles long and four miles wide. They also brought in a stamp mill to treat the quartz from the Phillips Lode, so rich that it was simply opened up much like a quarry. The vein ran from twenty-five to sixty feet wide. Stansell, who had been a theater doorman in Oro City, became the richest man in the diggings for a few years.

By September of 1860 all of the land in the district was taken up, and 2,000 men were working the area. Many of them had come over Mosquito Pass from California Gulch or had come from the Gregory diggings. Within a year eight steam-powered stamp mills and a dozen arrastras were in use for the crushing of ore. One of the best-known and best-preserved of these old arrastras is located by the edge of Buckskin Creek, two or three miles above the town site.

An arrastra, often used in Mexico and South America, was a crude device for crushing ore, but it had the advantage of being cheap and simple to construct for one-man operations. In a stone basin, eight to twelve feet in diameter, "mullers" (heavy rocks) were fastened to a horizontal arm and wheel. Either a mule or a man walked around the arrastra to turn the wheel, or water power occasionally was used. Water running through the arrastra washed away the unwanted rock and gravel. Often pieces of pure silver were found with the gold in the Buckskin arrastras.

(Although there are legends that Spaniards actually built some of the "Spanish" arrastras at Buckskin, there is no evidence to prove that any of these were built prior to 1860. Similar rumors that caves on the east side of Buckskin Gulch were the

75

hiding place of Spanish treasure and bandits' booty also seem unfounded.)

Because the crushing of ore in an arrastra was slow and laborious, stamp mills were preferred. The stamps were steam-powered iron shafts which pounded the rock to crush it. Some gold was caught in mercury and some was settled out much as in a sluice.

Over in the "Snow Blind District of Gilpin" in 1860 there was a short-lived camp called Eugene City, located above Montgomery Falls on the South Platte. Diggings extended above Eugene City as far as the snow line permitted.

These, then, were the beginnings of mining in South Park: Hamilton, Tarryall, Jefferson City, Nelson's Bar, Snow Blind and Eugene City, Buckskin, Pound Diggings, and "Fair Play." Of these earliest diggings only Fairplay has survived to become a permanent town.

CHAPTER FIVE

Mining: 1861-1870

In 1860 about 11,000 Americans had converged upon South Park, most of them being men. In all of Colorado in that year there were about 48,000 people. When the snows of the long, unusually severe winter of 1860-61 finally melted away, about 8,000 or 10,000 prospectors returned to work the placers of South Park; but in the entire Territory of Colorado the population reached only a little over 25,000. Thus, while the activity in the territory as a whole decreased, the importance of South Park increased proportionally in 1861.

Transportation was an important part of the life of the mining camps. The Central Overland California and Pikes Peak Express Company was running two coaches a week from Denver to Tarryall while the Kansas City Express had a weekly run from Denver on through to Buckskin Joe. William McClelland had charge of the Denver and South Park Stage Line. When activity became greater in Buckskin than in Tarryall in 1861, McClelland transferred the stage offices to Buckskin.

(Later in the 1860's McClelland left and Robert J. Spotswood, formerly an Indian fighter for Ben Holladay who owned the stage line, became superintendent. After 1865 McClelland and Spotswood together owned the South Park Stage Lines including the franchises of Hughes and Company, Wells-Fargo and Company, and Barlow-Sanderson and Company. In 1877 they extended the

Denver and South Park Stage Lines to Leadville but quit the business shortly after the railroads reached that booming town.)

Travelers and freighters into the mining district depended heavily on toll roads. In addition to the original roads, the Territorial Legislature authorized two more toll roads in the fall of 1861. One of these was the Park Junction, Georgia, and French Gulch Road Company which operated from Jefferson and Georgia Gulch to French Gulch. The other was the Breckenridge, Buckskin Joe and Hamilton Wagon Road Company operating between Breckenridge and Buckskin Joe, over Hoosier Pass, with a branch by way of Montgomery, Little French Gulch, and Tarryall Creek to Hamilton.

In 1862 the Ute Pass Wagon Road Company built the Colorado and Tarryall Road from Colorado City, while the Tarryall and Arkansas River Wagon Road Company laid out the California Gulch Road from Fairplay over Weston Pass to California Gulch. In 1866 the South Park, Blue River, and Middle Park Wagon Road Company entered the business, as did the Hamilton and Montgomery Wagon Road Company which took over the old route from Tarryall up to Deadwood and Little French Gulch to Montgomery.

The roads in the western and southern portions of the park, away from the busy mining districts to the north, could be lonely affairs, reminders that civilization in the mountains was spotty at best. Along the road south from Fairplay to Canon City, near the point where the Weston Pass road joined it, a character named Jonathan Leaper built a cabin in 1862. Leaper's hermitage, inviting to footsore and lonely prospectors on the trails from Weston and Trout Creek Passes, was in fact a snare for unsuspecting quarry.

Leaper looked the rogue that he was. Described as being six feet tall with a hulking frame, Leaper's small, deep-set eyes peered like snakes' eyes from under a low forehead. A woolly, black beard concealed the rest of his face, including the evil leer that undoubtedly lurked about his mouth. He seldom spoke to people who paused at his property, although they sometimes heard his laugh, like a maniac's, ringing through the treetops.

One poor fellow who rode across from California Gulch on an autumn day in 1862 stopped at ask Leaper for directions to the Denver road. Leaper told him to wait until morning when he personally could show him to the road, and graciously offered the traveler overnight accommodations. When the guest emerged from the dank hovel the next morning, he had been relieved of his gold, and his feet were tied securely beneath the mule on which he rode. Leaper's victim rode around South Park in this strait for three days before he was rescued by a woodcutter. The prospector died later.

When the episode was reported, U. S. Marshal Farnham set out to capture the guilty one in South Park. Disguised as a hungry prospector, the marshal bravely walked up to Leaper's door. Leaper, who had been joined in the meantime by a band of cohorts, invited him in, unburdened him of a blanket, a watch, and sundries, and threw him out.

The dauntless marshal returned, begging for food; and, when he was admitted, he succeeded in capturing Leaper. Leaper was taken to jail in Denver but was released in accordance with that town's method of saving on costs of board for prisoners. However, some of Denver's citizens thought that the streets would be safer if he left town, so they fired a few shots into the air to let him think that a necktie party was gathering. But someone else thought that a prisoner was escaping and shot him. Wounded, Leaper was taken back to jail. After his recovery he departed for Montana where he later was hanged for his supposed part in robbing an Indian agency there.

But South Park also had more conventional, though raw, stage stations which provided meals and overnight accommodations, changes of horses for stages, wood, and water. Among the earliest of the stations was Slaght's Ranch east of Kenosha Pass, a regular overnight stop for coaches from Denver. In existence at least by 1864 was Kenosha House on the west side of Kenosha Pass. In 1871 Mr. and Mrs. French were running a pleasant, neat hostelry there. The long house and barns, still operating as a station at the end of the decade, were liberally decorated with antlers on the outside and newspapers on the inside. It was then run by the Brubakers.

Case Stage Station was located at the western foot of this pass, and Michigan House was on Michigan Creek between Kenosha and Hamilton. One of the earliest, Eight-Mile House, was located at Tarryall Creek two miles east of the later town of Como. Built in 1860, it was still in existence in 1880.

Much of the traffic continued on across South Park and over the Mosquito Range. Late in the summer of 1861 the Central Overland Company inaugurated stage and mail service over 13,185-foot Weston Pass, with "Pony" Duncan delivering the weekly mail. This pass, which continued to be a well-used summer route through the 1860's and 1870's, was to be maintained by three different toll companies during those years. The pass was named for pioneers who ranched at both the eastern foot and the western foot of the range in the 1860's.

To meet the increasing needs of this influx of people, a duly constituted government was finally set up in 1861. Colorado had been part of the Territory of Kansas (officially) since 1854 and had become the Territory of Jefferson (unofficially) in 1859. When the Territory of Colorado was formally created in 1861, nine counties were established by the First Assembly in August. One of these was Park County, within which South Park lies. However, the legislature of Jefferson Territory had already created Park County in 1860 in January and had proclaimed Tarryall City as the "capital" of the county in November.

The first representative elected by Park County to the legislature of the Territory of Colorado was Wilbur Fisk Stone. Having spent the first twenty-seven years of his life moving farther and farther west, he had finally arrived at Tarryall in 1860. During his migration he had become a lawyer and a newspaper writer. His early career in Colorado included three years as Park County representative and four as the Assistant United States District Attorney before he left South Park to settle in Pueblo. There he was a lawyer and one of he first editors of the Pueblo *Chieftain*, prior to his being elected to the Supreme Court of Colorado.

Daniel Witter, the brother-in-law of Schuyler Colfax, also was

Montgomery and Mt. Lincoln were drawn to illustrate George W. Pine's travel account *Beyond the West*. Apparently, the artist thought that beyond the West lay Fujiyama. The two figures crowning the summit are undoubtedly George Pine and Mr. Myers of Montgomery who guided him to the top. *Courtesy, Denver Public Library Western Collection.*

William H. Jackson's camera sacrificed romance for realism in a picture of Mt. Lincoln and the valley that cradled Montgomery. *Courtesy, Library, State Historical Society.*

Montgomery as photographed by George D. Wakely, probably in 1864. *Courtesy, Denver Public Library Western Collection.*

The Falls of the Middle Fork of the South Platte River were utilized
for power and the timber of the surrounding hills stripped for construction
of cabins and flumes to arrastras, as seen in this 1867 photo by Chamberlain.
Courtesy, State Historical Society of Colorado.

A closer view of an arrastra and flume at Montgomery Falls. *Courtesy, Library, State Historical Society of Colorado.*

The Myers, a "refined English family," remained in Montgomery after the first wave of miners left in the late 1860's. The Myers made their income by running a hostelry for Eastern tourists who appreciated their little oasis of civilization. *Courtesy, Denver Public Library Western Collection.*

Montgomery in the 1870's, after the second wave of mining revived the town and resulted in the building of two refineries. *Courtesy, Denver Public Library Western Collection.*

Mt. Lincoln, 14,284 feet high, soars above Colorado Springs' Montgomery Dam, built on the site of the old mining town to store Blue River water which has been diverted through the Continental Divide at Hoosier Pass. *Colorado Springs Utilities Department photo.*

85

Jack trains became the usual transportation of supplies into the high mountain mines and of ore down the steep narrow slopes. *Courtesy, South Park City collection.*

High on Mt. Bross, the Moose Mine was the first silver mine of consequence to be found in South Park. It was opened up in 1871 and set off the second great wave of mining activity in the park. *Courtesy, South Park City collection.*

Remains of mines still found on Mt. Lincoln are eerie reminders of the harsh, lonely lives of the miners who worked them, often year round. *John Kuglin photo.*

The Moose Mining Company's office, pictured here, and a smelter were located at the town of Dudley, a mile and a half above Alma. *George White photo.*

When Alma sprang up in the early 1870's, it was a supply town for the mining districts around Mt. Bross, but more importantly it became the center of smelting for silver ores from mines of the vicinity. In this photo, taken in the 1870's, the branch works of the Boston and Chicago Smelting Company are in full operation with a battlement of cordwood ready for the furnaces. *Courtesy of the Denver Public Library Western Collection.*

When the miners came to town, Alma's main street became the parking area for their faithful burros, who waited patiently while the owners had "one for the trail." *Courtesy of the South Park City collection.*

An unusually quiet day on Alma's main street in the 1880's is watched over by Mt. Bross in the background. *Courtesy of the Denver Public Library Western Collection, James W. Nutt photo.*

The charming lady bedecked with the ammunition belt is said to be Annie Oakley, visiting Alma "with friends" in 1883. Is it Annie or isn't it? *Courtesy of the Denver Public Library Western Collection.*

Alma survived as an active town well into the 1900's. These buildings are still standing in the town which, though dozing today, is far from dead. *Courtesy of the Denver Public Library Western Collection, L. C. McClure photo.*

89

A view of the Dolly Varden Mill looking down toward the South Platte shows the ore buckets which were emptied into the large round bin. *Courtesy of the Denver Public Library Western Collection, L. C. McClure photo.*

The Dolly Varden Mill was located between Dudley and Montgomery on the old road which parallels Colorado 9. The concrete foundations of the structure are all that remain today. *Courtesy of the Denver Public Library Western Collection, L. C. McClure photo.*

This miner's cabin, well-insulated and braced against wintry blasts, is on a ridge of Mt. Sherman near the Sacramento Mine. The view is taken toward Hoosier Pass to the north. *Vaun Benjamin photo.*

The town of Sacramento was below timberline, down the mountain from the mine. This skeleton is the ruins of Sacramento's two-storied boarding-house. *Vaun Benjamin photo.*

91

This aerial view of the Mosquito Range shows the group of peaks which extends south of Fairplay with Horseshoe Mountain's glacial cirque rising above Horseshoe Gulch and Fourmile Creek. The mountains are, from left to right, Sheep Mountain, Horseshoe Mountain and Horseshoe Pass, Mt. Sheridan, and Mt. Sherman. *U. S. Geological Survey, T. S. Lovering photo.*

The Hilltop Mine was the big producer in the Horseshoe district and has been worked in recent years. *John Kuglin photo.*

Looking down through Leavick in the 1890's, one can make out one tram tower behind the stable. The little cabins in Leavick at this time were all log. *Courtesy of the Library, State Historical Society of Colorado, photo from J. G. Jack's* Pikes Peak, Plum Creek and South Platte Forest Reserve.

This fine view of deserted Leavick was taken in the 1920's. Notice that the log cabins have been replaced with houses built of lumber. Sheep Mountain rises behind the shoulder of Mt. Sheridan. *Carl Mathews photo.*

The Leavick mill in the 1920's. *Carl Mathews photo.*

The Leavick mill again is seen looking toward Horseshoe Mountain. The mill was the only building at Leavick in the 1960's. *Courtesy of the South Park City collection.*

The Weston Pass road was used heavily in 1878 and 1879 for hauling freight to Leadville and for bringing ore and bullion out of the fabulous mining town. Here, sixty-five tons of silver bullion and ten tons of ore are being well guarded at Platte Station, a stage station at the eastern foot of Weston Pass. *Courtesy of the Library, State Historical Society of Colorado.*

elected to the Territorial Legislature in 1861. Witter was thirty-two when he bought up a claim in Tarryall in 1859. Before coming to Colorado, he had taught in normal schools in Indiana, had operated a book and stationery shop, and had studied law. After spending the winter of 1859-60 in Indiana with his family, he returned and became the postmaster of Hamilton in 1860. He spent his spare time mining. He caught a beaver in his flume one day and planned to keep it as a mascot for the post office, but the beaver was brought to a quick end after chewing the leg off a table.

By the spring of 1861, Witter was ready to give up "batching," and he sent for his wife Clara and their two children. They traveled from Indiana by rail as far as Eddyville, Iowa, the end of track, where Daniel met them. The family then came by light wagon, covering the 500 miles to Denver in a month. From Denver into the mountains, they took the Bradford Road, camping out the first night at "Bradford Cave," better known as Colorow's Cave.

At Hamilton Clara had to adapt to the rough conditions of a raw mining camp. To her dismay, there were no potatoes—only beans. The only fruit was dried apples and mountain berries, so she learned to make mince meat from the dried fruit and antelope meat.

Her house was a two-room cabin. One room, with the luxury of a board floor, served as kitchen, diningroom, and bedroom, while the other, with a dirt floor, was the post office and livingroom. Here the miners came to inquire for letters and to buy stamps and tobacco. Since the Witters weighed gold dust for payment from these miners, they also took care to sweep the floor once a week and to wash the sweepings to collect a little extra income from the dust.

Indians, who occasionally lingered around the post office, called Mrs. Witter "Sam" because her husband worked for Uncle Sam. Once they alarmed her by stealing her wash from the line while Witter was gone to California Gulch. When someone shouted for help, the Utes scurried south into the park where the settlers and the Indians exchanged a few rifle shots as a formality.

A Mrs. Duncan was the only other woman in Hamilton, according to Clara Witter's account. However, a Mrs. Curtiss lived two and a half miles up the Tarryall, so on Sundays the Witters would go visiting the Curtisses. But the mining camp offered few of these nice diversions for genteel family life. After only a year in Hamilton, the Witters moved to Denver, where Daniel became a tax assessor after serving his term in the legislature. There the Witters raised eleven children.

Despite the lack of comforts which Clara Witter had missed, Hamilton was a lively commercial center and crossroad in 1861. Thirteen hydraulic operations were being worked in addition to the more usual sluices. Dunbar's Hotel was full and newcomers were arriving daily. There were several other hotels, stores, express offices, and even the Olympic Opera House; and freighters from Denver, Colorado City, and Canon City were kept busy hauling in provisions for the district.

Since gold dust and nuggets served as exchange for the prospectors, in 1861 Dr. John Parsons began to mint coins to provide more convenient currency. Parsons had come to Tarryall Diggings from Illinois in 1859. His gold pieces were minted in $2.50 and $5 denominations. These coins had an eagle on one side encircled by the words "Pike's Peak Gold" and the denomination. On the other side was a stamp mill and the words "J. Parson [sic] and Co., Oro." Parsons considered moving his mint to Buckskin at one time, but by 1864 the mint was no longer in existence because of the Government's prohibition of private minting.

In 1861 South Park had its first newspaper when William N. Byers, John L. Dailey, Edward Bliss, and H. E. Rounds began weekly publication of the *Miners' Record* at Tarryall. It was published only from July 4 of that year until September 14 when the miners began again to drift away for the winter.

However, there were enough prospectors remaining to have a Christmas Eve ball at Hemphill and Duke's International Hall in Hamilton. After the ball a supper was served at Robinson's

Saloon. The affair was such a success that it was followed by a New Year's dance at Winthrop and Cotton's hall. But the heyday of the Tarryall Diggings had ended with the summer of 1861, although the hum of summertime activity would continue for a few more years.

On the other hand, Fairplay was becoming established as a permanent town. The camp had first gained attention when rates were published for gold dust being circulated for exchange. Whereas common retorted gold was worth twelve dollars an ounce, and the best retorted gold was worth fifteen dollars, Fairplay Gulch gold was said to be worth seventeen dollars. Furthermore, the moraines and bars along the Platte River promised to yield mineral for a long time.

Starting in 1859 as "Fair Play," the camp shortly had become "Fairplay Diggings" and then in 1861 "Platte City." Then it again became "Fairplay" until 1869 when the name was officially changed to "South Park City." In 1874 the name "Fairplay" was restored.

One of the early prospectors in Fairplay was William Coleman, who owned most of what became the town site as he sold off land. By 1861 about 100 people lived at Fairplay, and the Winslow House had been built. With the Platte River diverted into ditches to permit hydraulic mining, the diggings attracted nearly 250 miners in the following summer, the men earning anywhere from five to twenty-five dollars a day.

Early Fairplay had its full share of violence. In 1860 two Texans, Pemly and Sanford, met at the camp and avenged a matter of family honor in a duel. Sanford had ruined Pemly's sister and then fled from Texas. Pemly pursued the villain to Australia, New Zealand, Canada, and California before he finally caught up with him at Fairplay. There the two met with rifles at thirty paces, and Sanford was shot through the heart by his one-time school chum. Pemly was acquitted of the murder charge that was later filed against him.

Two years hence another murder occurred in Fairplay when a Henry MacKay killed Alex Ross for some forgotten and, undoubtedly, less romantic cause.

Needless to say, the wild and woolly mining camps were of great concern to the churches back in the shelter of civilization. Following William Howbert's circuit ministry, the Methodists sent John Dyer to serve its South Park Mission. Through the 1860's and 1870's Dyer was to labor in the camps of South Park and in the neighboring regions, covering much of his large circuit on foot or, in the winter, on long Norwegian skis. For this practice he became known as the "snowshoe itinerant." Mining for gold and carrying mail to stretch out his meager income, he held services wherever he could muster a congregation.

Dyer's life always was marked by hardship and tragedy. Following the death of his first wife, Dyer had entered an unfortunate marriage which ended in divorce and the wife's subsequent death, evidently a suicide. Dogged by feelings of guilt and remorse, Dyer entered the Methodist ministry in Wisconsin in 1851. He came to Denver in June of 1861. Trading a watch there for $20, with which he was able to buy supplies, he set out on foot for South Park and arrived in Buckskin in July. In August he went to Fairplay and there preached to thirty. Although his flock at Fairplay never was large, he was able to bring together twenty-five in the middle of the next winter when he held services at Sharman's Store.

Catholic worship also was held in Fairplay in the earliest years by Father Joseph Machebeuf. This French priest had been sent to Denver from New Mexico in 1860. By September of 1861 he had made eight trips to South Park, and he continued these pastoral visits until mining declined in 1864. He again returned and held mass in Fairplay and Buckskin Joe in 1867 and 1868. Although he visited Hamilton and Montgomery also at that time, there were not enough parishioners left in those camps by then to have a mass.

Just as Fairplay showed evidence of becoming a permanent town, the Beaver Creek placers nearby were also settling into long-term mining. These placers, located on the creek which runs parallel to Highway 9 between Fairplay and Alma but hidden to view by an intervening ridge east of the road, were worked through most of the remaining years of the 1800's and then were dredged in the 1900's.

The original owner of the Beaver Creek placers, Daniel Pound, sold his claims to Freeman and Pease. In 1862 a ditch and a flume a mile long were built. A large interest in this operation was sold in 1866 to the Pennsylvania Gold and Silver Mining Company, a group of Philadelphia investors.

In 1861 about 300 miners returned to neighboring Buckskin, and mining remained active, with the Phillips alone producing $500,000 in 1861 and 1862. And as far as the miners were concerned, the name of the camp still was Buckskin despite the fact that it had been changed to Laurette in 1860 to honor the wives of Miles and Allen Dodge—Laura and Jeanette.

By 1861 the town had a steam sawmill, and the Drug and Yankee Notion Store was opened by Ware, Morey and Company. C. W. Kitchen had come from Canon City to open a store in Buckskin, as well as his others at California Gulch, Georgetown, and Kelly's Bar. With thirty eight-mule teams Kitchen hauled goods to these stores in the mining camps from Kansas City for three years.

A *Rocky Mountain News* correspondent in November, 1861, reported that the town's stores were being stocked for the coming winter; and "We think we have as fine a group of families and nice ladies as to be found anywhere, and enjoy as good society as any in the country." There were, indeed, several families at Buckskin, and the first white child born in Park County drew his initial gasp of mountain air in that town.

However, Buckskin's fame was not for family living. Rather, it gained an early reputation for the more sensational variety of entertainment and crimes. There were as many people working in saloons and dance halls as there were in mining, and Harris's Theater had a Negro minstrel group strumming the hours away until dawn.

One of the dance hall girls was Silver Heels. (Although different versions of the Silver Heels story place her at Fairplay, Alma, or Leadville, most agree that she danced at Buckskin, arriving there in 1861 and living in a cabin across the creek from town.) She arrived in town one day on the stagecoach, veiled and wearing slippers with silver heels. Walking into Billy Buck's saloon, she got a job when she removed her veil to reveal the most beautiful face ever seen in the camps. Her fame and popularity as a dancer became unmatched.

Who she was, no one knew. One story claims that she was a Moravian girl named Girda Bechtel who had hired out to come West from Pennsylvania to help a widow with her children. At Denver Girda's aspirations for a theatrical career prompted her to leave the widow and to accept lessons as a dancer and singer. Eventually she arrived in Buckskin, ready to test her talents in the roaring camp.

However, two Mexicans, driving sheep through the region, brought a smallpox epidemic to the town. As miner after miner was stricken, Silver Heels faithfully cared for them until she too contracted the disease. When the epidemic had passed, the miners took up a purse to show their gratitude to her. But they found Silver Heels' cabin deserted when they arrived with the gift. No one knows what became of her. The legend claims that her face had been so disfigured by the pox that she stole away to anonymity but that a shadowy, veiled figure—thought to be Silver Heels—was sometimes seen visiting a grave in the cemetery. The miners, determined to pay some tribute to the dance hall girl, then named a nearby, solitary peak Mount Silverheels. This name does, indeed, appear on maps by the middle 1860's.

To this heathen paradise Father Dyer had come. When Dyer first arrived in July, 1861, William Howbert still was officially in charge of the circuit. However, in August Dyer himself began to preach in the camps. At Buckskin he held services in the only place available—a gambling hall.

Father Dyer preached in Buckskin at intervals in the following years. In January of 1862 he "held Meetings" there for two weeks "in the face of every kind of opposition"—such as, two balls a week, Professor Fornia's dancing institute, a theater, two murders; "and yet, notwithstanding all these things, we had a good meeting."

On his way to Buckskin on that occasion, Dyer had come

over Weston Pass from the Arkansas Valley in the dead of winter. Dyer always chose his routes for mileage rather than for climate. During that January trek, Dyer found himself in a storm. Wading through snow waist deep and unable to light a fire because of wet matches, he kept going. He had decided that if his strength gave out, he would calmly sit down to die, writing his own epitaph on a tree: "Look for me in heaven." However, he found the Weston Pass toll gate in the dark night, and the Swedish gatekeeper there gave him shelter. After holding the meeting in Buckskin, Dyer set out in February on a 100-mile trip to Denver—walking to save the stage fare of $10.

By 1862 Stansell, Harris, and Bond had extended their activities to owning a bank in Buckskin where they were "Dealers in Gold Dust, Coin, and Exchange." The town also had four hotels in 1862—the Cherokee, the O.K. House, the Pacific House and the Laurette House and Hall. There were two dance halls. Gun fights and the gay life were the order of the day—and night.

Among the people living in Buckskin at that time, Horace and Augusta Tabor could be counted as part of the respectable citizenry. After running a store and doing some prospecting at Oro City for a year, they had come to Buckskin Joe in the fall of 1861 and opened a store. This store became the post office with Tabor serving as the postmaster of "Laurette" from 1863 until 1868, the name being changed back to Buckskin in February, 1866. In addition, Tabor had a store in Montgomery and was the superintendent of schools for Park County. Augusta kept boarders, and Horace grubstaked prospectors, as he would do at Leadville. There he would grubstake August Rische and George Hooke with whom he shared one-third interest in the Little Pittsburgh, which made his fortune. The Tabors remained at Buckskin until 1868, two or three years after activity had dropped off in the district. When they left the deserted camp, they returned to Oro City where fortune, fame, and scandal were to come to them in the Leadville bonanza in 1878.

Interest in politics was lively in Buckskin. In December of 1861 the first county election was held with 382 votes being cast. A meeting of the elected county commissioners was set for January 6 in Fairplay. When one of the commissioners had still failed to arrive by the evening of January 7, the other two met, appointed county officers, and voted to move the "capital" of Park County to Laurette since that town had polled most of the votes in the December election.

A week later all three commissioners met at the new county seat. Taxes were levied for schools, for the territory, and for the county; and a poll tax of fifty cents per man was set. Six precincts were created: at Slaghts Ranch east of Kenosha Pass, at Hamilton, at Fairplay, at Montgomery, at Laurette, and at Mosquito.

In March, 1862, a newspaper with political overtones began publication in Buckskin. Matt Riddlebarger and L. B. St. James had purchased the Tarryall *Miners' Record,* moved it to Buckskin, and there published the paper as the *Western Mountaineer.* Printed weekly only until December of the same year, the newspaper's life was shortened by the Confederate sympathies of its owners.

The issue of Unionist and Secessionist loyalties provoked lively concern in the mining camps, where street fights between proponents of the opposing views became regular Saturday night fare. About one third of the people in the new Territory of Colorado were Southern sympathizers in 1861; and Confederate leaders in the South hoped to win over the territories of Colorado, New Mexico, and Utah as well as California, thus controlling all of the regions in which gold was being produced.

In February of 1861 Texas had seceded from the Union and in July sent troops into New Mexico, and in October a group of Colorado men with Confederate loyalties went down the Arkansas to eastern Colorado and there attempted to form a fighting unit. When the small force of men was arrested, it was found to include men from Tarryall, Fairplay, and Georgia Gulch as well as from the Gilpin district. As Confederate activity increased, by December Colorado volunteers were being mustered to go to Fort Union in New Mexico to reinforce the strength of that post.

Governor Gilpin quickly organized some three thousand volunteers to send to New Mexico. Company C of the army was made up of men chiefly from Denver City and Buckskin Joe

104

while Company E's enlistees were from Oro City and Buckskin. Gilpin's volunteers met the Confederates at Glorieta Pass in New Mexico in March, 1862, and halted any further threat to the gold territories with a decisive victory there. Company E with about seventy men won the distinction of dealing the crucial blow to defeat the Confederates, while Company C was fated to suffer the most casualties.

It is not surprising, then, to find feelings running high as summer approached in the South Park mining camps in 1862. However, there were no reports of organized violence despite a rumor printed in the *Western Mountaineer* in August that "100 Seceshers" were about to take over Fairplay.

By August one of the owners of the newspaper was complaining to Colonel John Francisco, a candidate for election to Congress, that the *Mountaineer* was about to expire because Francisco and his friends had failed to send money promised to keep the paper going. It was running in the red as Unionists boycotted the sheet and its editorial policy. In September Colonel Francisco himself came to the district campaigning. He met Captain Hamilton, the Republican candidate, for a political debate in Liggett's Hall at Montgomery. Posters announcing the event had been carried on teams through the camps. But, although the hall was filled, "with the exception of a mule load from Buckskin, Democrats were very scarce." After the election, which gave a strong victory to the Unionists, the *Western Mountaineer* folded.

However, one might deduce that some Confederate activity continued with the encouragement of the owners of the Phillips Lode. With Stansell as captain, a Volunteer Company of Infantry was organized at Buckskin in February of 1863. Called the "Buckskin Greys," the officers had a uniform of grey shirts and trousers, although the enlisted men merely had grey shirts to wear with their own overalls and hats. Ostensibly, the company was raised for protection against Indians and bandits. Perhaps the matter was that simple, in which case the organizers were singularly injudicious in their choice of uniforms.

Across the long, sharp ridge of Loveland Mountain lay the Mosquito Mining District, where life was considerably quieter.

The district was four miles to the southwest of Buckskin Gulch and had resulted from the overflow of miners from Buckskin in 1861. The first discovery recorded in Mosquito Gulch was the Newland Lode, found in June, 1861. Then in July John Smith, Joseph Pollock, William Cadwell, and James Newland staked out and recorded the Sterling Lode. The Lulu Lode and Orphan Boy discoveries soon brought a wave of prospectors into the district. The Orphan Boy was to become one of the most important gold producers in Park County in a later period.

Early in the summer the Mosquito Mining District was organized; but, according to Father Dyer's account, the initial meeting adjourned without the miners' having agreed upon a name. When the men next met, it is said, a well-pressed mosquito was found between the pages of the minutes of the previous meeting—exactly on the blank spot where a name was to be filled in. Thus the problem of a name was solved. (However, a diligent but unsportsmanlike reporter for the *Rocky Mountain News* thoroughly examined the books in 1862 and failed to find even the faintest anopheline smudge.)

In September the town of Sterling in the Mosquito District was laid out. This town, sometimes called Sterling City, but usually and informally called Mosquito, was just west of Park City, a slightly later town much of which is still standing about a mile and a half west of Alma. Mosquito was near the Orphan Boy Mine. A Vermonter, Nathan Hurd, brought a twelve-stamp mill into the district and built the wagon road into the town.

When Father Dyer preached in the camp in August, 1861, he found no houses there as yet. He himself built a shelter of poles and pine boughs and lived there for two months. During that period he hired out as a miner.

John Smith—former squaw man, trapper, Denver merchant, co-discoverer of the Sterling Lode, and owner of a quartz mill in Sterling—met Samuel Leach in Denver in 1862 and persuaded him to go to Sterling to run a store which Smith was opening. Smith built a two-storied store building and petitioned for a post office. The 250 citizens of the district had been getting their mail from the Laurette post office until then. Postal service was finally established in 1863.

In the meantime Leach was running the business and reported in a letter that, contrary to most of the mining camps, Sterling had no murders, lynchings, or gambling. Instead, the men occupied themselves with cards (not played for money), with quoits, wrestling, boxing, shooting matches, and horseback riding. By 1863 the peaceful camp was becoming too quiet, though, as the prospectors began to drift away to Montana and Idaho mines or back East to fight in the war. The town struggled along, however, with Leach still operating the store until 1866.

During those years much of Dyer's activities centered around Mosquito and the high mountain pass to the west. In 1863 he was preaching on his circuit three times on Sunday and once or twice during the week. He spent his other days prospecting. For almost a month that year he worked Pennsylvania Gulch, west of Mosquito, since the claims there had been abandoned. He simply took temporary possession of an empty thirty-six by fifteen-foot boardinghouse and moved in. The building had one large room with six bedsteads with poles for springs. Unsuccessful both in prospecting and in sleeping on the poles, Dyer returned to Mosquito.

However, before the winter was out, Dyer was hard-pressed for enough money for his living. During the summer flour had cost $5 a sack in the town of Mosquito. By the end of the winter supplies were so scarce that the same amount of flour cost $40. With church contributions even lower than usual, Dyer decided to take a contract in February, 1864, to carry the mail in addition to his church duties. Once a week for $18 he walked or skied the lonely route from Buckskin and Mosquito over Mosquito Pass to Oro City and Granite. He also carried gold dust sometimes for miners.

Mosquito Pass, which was to become famous in the early years of the Leadville boom, was little more than a chip on the soaring rim of the Mosquito Range. The pass itself lay at 13,188 feet. The climb involved a sharp ascent out of Mosquito Gulch around London Hill to American Flats. Above the flats lay another steep climb to the barren, wind-swept summit of the pass. From the notch on a clear day the view extended all the way to Pikes Peak on the east and beyond the spine of the Rockies, the Sawatch Range, to Mount Sopris on the west. The descent down the western side of the pass was so steep that the narrowest track with sharp switchbacks was all that could be constructed when a stage road was built in later years.

The crossings of this alpine trail by Dyer have become legendary. Using skis about ten feet long, Dyer carried loads of about thirty pounds on his back. The depth of snow varied on the route from three to twenty feet. The winter of 1863-64 was an unusually long one, lingering until June. Since there were no cabins all the way from Mosquito to California Gulch, Dyer could expect no shelter or assistance along the way. Often though, he aided others whom he found in trouble. One whom he saved from freezing was a few years later the leader of a mob that murdered Dyer's son, a judge, in his courtroom at Granite. Dyer carried the mail on the Mosquito Pass route for five months.

Dyer was again living in a cabin in Mosquito during the winter of 1865-66 while he preached in the neighboring districts. In the 1870's about thirty people still lived in the town. By 1900 it was empty.

North of the Mosquito and Buckskin districts another camp developed. It was the Independent District, laid out on the northeast shoulder of Mt. Bross in July, 1861. The *Miners' Record* in August of 1861 said that the Putnam Lode, a quartz lode, had been discovered in July and that several arrastras were under construction there. Also, in August Father Dyer preached to about thirty people at the location, which he called Quartz Hill although it usually has been known as Quartzville. The town was on a level bench near timberline about a mile and a half directly east of Mt. Cameron. Its site possesses some of the most breath-taking scenery to be found anywhere in an area where the spectacular is commonplace.

In the valley far below Quartzville lay Montgomery. In August of 1861 the Snow Blind Mining District had been re-organized as the Montgomery District. When Dyer went there during that month, he found that everyone was out staking claims with the exception of one man. That one hospitably invited Dyer to eat with him—on the ground in the absence of any house or table. But a town quickly sprang up when twenty new lodes, including the rich Pendleton Lode, were opened. The town itself was in the basin where Montgomery Dam Reservoir now is located, but many of the workings and cabins were above the town, along and behind the waterfall, where the Magnolia Mill was located.

By the fall of 1861 the town of Montgomery had two hotels, one with a public hall in the upper floor, and seventy cabins. There were two sawmills, and Robert Olds had come in from Canon City to open a store. The loyal citizens met and voted to name the towering, mineral-rich peak to the west Mt. Lincoln and sent a bar of its gold to the President.

In 1862 the population of Montgomery leaped to a thousand. Six quartz mills were operating. The town had a drugstore, Ware and Morey's mercantile store, a dry-goods emporium, and assorted hotels and saloons. Pony Duncan was running the mail to Buckskin daily while the Overland Express maintained weekly service to Denver even through the winter. Despite the fact that the Methodists and Presbyterians held weekly meetings, taking turns in arranging the services, Montgomery had, by the summer of 1863, gained a name as one of the rowdier camps. Even winter snows that reached to the tops of the doors failed to put a damper on Montgomery.

When Bayard Taylor, a clergyman from New Jersey on a lecture tour, visited the town in 1866, he found a population of 300 to 400. Taylor supposed that, since Montgomery showed no signs of decay (in fact, the town seemed to be growing some), the rest of the buildings of the once-roaring camp had been burned as firewood. Taylor addressed an audience of 100 at the town, after which he observed that whereas the "ignorant adventurers" had drifted away, "those remaining were of refinement and education."

Taylor also visited Fairplay, which he found to be a "quiet little place" with about 200 residents in 1866. He stayed at James Castello's log hotel. "Genial" Judge Castello had been born at

Florissant, Missouri, and had come to Colorado in 1860. He went first to the Gregory Diggings and then to Fairplay. In 1863 he sent for his wife and children and opened the hotel. He also became the justice of peace. In 1870 the family homesteaded a ranch and opened up another hotel at what was to become Florissant, Colorado.

In 1866 Fairplay had a brewery run by Charles and Leonard Sumner, making South Park Lager Beer. This same brewery stayed in operation, keeping its head above the depression that was settling over the South Park mining camps. When Leadville boomed in the late 1870's, the Sumner Brewery also was to thrive for a brief time as the sole beer supplier for its thirsty hordes of miners. The original wooden structure burned in 1873 and was replaced by a stone building which now houses a museum at the South Park City restoration in Fairplay.

Also, by 1866 Fairplay had a school which met in a log cabin. A Mr. McLean there taught about twenty-five pupils, some of whom came from outlying camps and boarded with Fairplay families. In 1867 Fairplay got the county seat, too. As Buckskin Joe dwindled, the records were moved to a one-room log cabin in Fairplay. This cabin stands today near the present stone Park County Courthouse.

Father Dyer went to Montgomery and bought an empty log hotel building which he arranged to have dragged to Fairplay for a church. Now he no longer had to hold services in a store under a sign reading "Good Whiskey."

Established as the center of activity in the region, the town had several stores, livery stables, hotels, and—of course—saloons. However, much of this early town was destroyed by fire in 1873.

Bayard Taylor made passing comment on two other locations of interest during his 1866 trip. He mentioned stopping at Dan's Ranche, four or five miles south of Hamilton. He described the place as a dirty, two-storied tavern owned by a German. Dan's Ranche was probably Dan McLaughlin's stage station. Leaving Dan's Ranche, Taylor continued on to the east, passing through the site of Jefferson. He reported that this place was completely abandoned.

Two years later, in 1868, the impressive entourage of the Honorable Schuyler Colfax progressed through the mountains of Colorado (see Chapter II). In the party, besides Colfax, were the Honorable William Bross, Lieutenant Governor of Illinois; Samuel Bowles, editor of the Springfield, Massachusetts, *Republican;* Bowles' daughter; the Matthews family, one of whom was the fiancée of Frank Hall; Miss Nellie Wade, the fiancée of Mr. Colfax; Governor A. C. Hunt of Colorado; and others blended to create a surrealistic picture of political rallies, Eastern drawing-room society, giggling sweethearts, professional journalism, uncomfortable mountain hotels, hysterics induced by nonexistent enemy Indians, and finally the arrival of Mrs. Dan Witter, sister of Schuyler Colfax, with her newest, squalling six-week-old baby. All this in *Bayou Salado.*

From Denver the party had gone to Central City, Georgetown, Breckenridge, and then South Park. Coming down Breckenridge Pass (later Boreas Pass) through Hamilton, the group found about fifty empty cabins, two log hotels, and about twenty people living in the once-bustling town. In his account of the trip, Bowles described it as a "grimy, dirty looking village . . . with manure heaps in front of the houses, and a few sorry looking horses and mules scattered about the pastures." (The following year when geologist William Brewer visited the section, he estimated that only a dozen people lived in the whole Tarryall district from Hamilton to Deadwood.)

At Montgomery the Colfax party found one or two hundred empty cabins but one family, the Myers, was still living there. They were "cultivated, tasteful" English people who gave them a square meal and a "hearty welcome." From Montgomery some of the hardier members of the group climbed Mt. Lincoln. Here Bross was so moved that he sang the Doxology, and the party in turn named the ponderous mountain to the south in his honor.

Going on to Fairplay, they found the town crowded with people who had come to hear Colfax and Bross speak. The group stayed at the crowded log hotel; but, when they returned through South Park from the Arkansas Valley districts a few weeks later, they elected to bypass the rude hotel for a pristine campsite a mile from Fairplay. It was at this time that the party experienced the Indian alarm described in an earlier chapter, so a Ute Indian escort kept guard in the woods nearby while the excursionists slept in their tents and bedrolls under the stars, enjoying their last night in the renowned *Bayou Salado* which they had come to see.

When William Brewer visited Buckskin in 1869 there were about thirty men left, but the town was nearly destroyed. Brewer wandered about the empty buildings—around Professor Du Bois' Assay Office where Du Bois had left his books, balances, and crucibles on the shelves. Du Bois was apparently still in the district. Brewer saw Stansell's weathering theater and his three little *maisons du plaisir,* for Stansell had continued to diversify his interests beyond mere mining and banking. The old roaring Buckskin was dead. For many years the stone chimney of the old courthouse, which remained a few years, stood as a sentinel; but it too was destroyed in 1936.

When Brewer stopped in Montgomery, he was accompanied on a climb to the summit of Mt. Lincoln by Mr. Myers. This climb had become something of a pilgrimage and a *coup* for Eastern tourists after Lincoln's assassination. At the time of Brewer's visit, the Myers' house was so full of travelers that his geological party slept in the abandoned "Colorado House."

In 1871 the Myers were still at Montgomery. The home was cozy and neat, Mrs. Myers having acquired a sewing machine and a cabinet organ, and Mr. Myers a roomful of skins for trade. Evidently both the summer tourist business and winter trapping had been good, and they were about to enjoy another mining boom as we shall see.

But the original wave of mining in South Park was finished. From 1860 to 1863 Park County had produced $1,500,000 in gold, surpassed by Summit, Lake, Gilpin, and Clear Creek Counties, in that order. Much of this earliest mining had been done in one-man operations which involved little capital. However, as milling came to involve more money, prospectors had borrowed with the result that increasingly mining properties had fallen into the hands of banks. After 1863, as the Civil War caused the price

112

of gold to advance, Eastern investors began to put money into these Colorado mines. Then a boom which occurred in mining stock collapsed, scaring off prospective investors in the mines.

Furthermore, the period from 1864 to 1868 was difficult for everyone in Colorado. There were troubles from drouth, from high wages, from the interruptions of Civil War and the Indian wars, from broken supply and communication lines. After the Civil War a national depression settled over the entire country and lifted but slowly. Furthermore, Colorado gold mining had been exaggerated and poor in comparison with the yield of the other Western territories in the early years. It would need a dramatic stimulus to renew interest and activity.

CHAPTER SIX

"In the Hands of Hard Men in an Evil Hour"

Criminals seem to disrupt and refuse to conform to classification in historical accounts. Such heroes as Kit Carson and Father Dyer obligingly meld into society's record of accomplishments, but the villainous Espinosas and the Reynolds Gang do not. In order to bring their stories into the period in which they occurred, we must digress from the mining account.

The first of these stories, that of the Espinosas, took place in 1863. It began not in South Park but in the San Luis Valley, when two Mexicans, Vivian and José Espinosa, determined to reap revenge on the Gringos. Whether the real cause of their hatred stemmed from immediate grievances, or whether it was part of a general animosity toward the American victors of the Mexican War who had taken possession of New Mexico, is beclouded in time. It is know that the Espinosa family had come to the San Luis Valley from New Mexico in the 1860's. Also, one story says that Americans ran off their sheep and killed a young boy in the family, after which brutality the Espinosas avenged themselves by killing some of the law men and ranchers who were responsible.

José and Vivian soon after headed north on the fantastic mission of killing as many Americans as possible, in the name of the Blessed Virgin. In March, 1863, the two came upon Judge William Bruce who was working alone at his sawmill on Hardscrabble Creek near Wetmore in the Canon City area. Bruce was the first victim of the Espinosas in Colorado. Next they moved toward the northeast to Little Fountain Creek where

114

they killed Henry Harkins, also operating an isolated sawmill. This site was about ten miles west of the town of Fountain, Colorado, and afterward was called Dead Man's Canyon.

The Espinosas headed west to South Park after this murder. Their route has been placed in Ute Pass where two men were found dead shortly after Harkins' slaying, but it is not certain that they went that way or killed the two men there. On the edge of the park they did murder a rancher named J. D. Addleman, the first of at least seven victims in the park.

A couple of days after the Addleman murder, they cut down two more men around Red Hill. One of these was a brother of Lieutenant George Shoup, prominent in South Park and in the Colorado Volunteers. The other was named Binkley, possibly the freighter from Hamilton.

The next sacrificial lamb was a prospector, Bill Carter, who was working his claim at the time near the site of Cottage Grove. The Espinosas robbed Carter's body of his gun, money, and clothing. Two days later Lehman and Seyga were killed in the rough country around Red Hill as they were returning to California Gulch on the road from Denver.

During this period no one was sure who the murderers were. It even was thought that Confederates had commenced guerrilla warfare in the area. All that was certain was that no one was safe alone out of doors, even with six cavalry men combing the park for the criminals. Any stranger became suspect. One fellow from California Gulch ran from Red Hill all the way to Fairplay to escape a posse which was on his trail. He was saved in Fairplay when Father Dyer saw him run into town, his shoes gone by then. Recognizing him, Dyer was able to rescue him only by shielding the man with his own body until they reached the protection of a house.

A more distressing incident occurred a few days later when word came to Fairplay that a strange man was being harbored in a house about fifteen miles east of town. A posse rode out to the farm and demanded his surrender. The family refused and, instead, fired some shots from the house, killing a mule. When the posse threatened to burn the house to drive them all out

115

into the open, the man gave himself up. The posse paused long enough to take some goods from the house to repay the loss of their mule and then took the prisoner to Fairplay where he was hanged without trial. The fellow's name was Baxter. Why he was hiding remains a mystery. Perhaps he was a Confederate, and Rebels were prime suspects in that hour.

Then one day a man named Metcalf was shot at as he was hauling lumber down the road from the Alma area to Fairplay. The bullet was stopped by a thick wad of papers in his breast pocket, a copy of the Emancipation Proclamation being among them. Metcalf saw two Mexicans, one of whom was taking aim for a second shot. However, Metcalf's ox team elected not to wait for another explosion from the gun. They were already making a dash for it down the road, and so Metcalf was able to escape. Reaching Fairplay, he told what had happened, and a posse of seventeen men organized immediately.

They followed the Espinosas down through the park. At the Addleman ranch one member of the posse, John Addleman, was left, as he had cracked under the strain of the summer's grim events. After several days of scouring the hills which rimmed the south end of the park, the volunteers found the Espinosa camp in the area around Fourmile Creek near Thirtynine Mile Mountain.

When José Espinosa appeared to ready a horse for riding, the posse killed him. In some confusion, they thought that Vivian was a member of their own group, and he thus escaped before his identity was clear.

Rewards were offered for the capture of the remaining member of the bloodthirsty pair. Tom Tobin, a mountain man living in the San Luis Valley, went after him in hopes of securing the reward. He found Vivian and a young nephew who had joined him hiding out in the Sangre de Cristo Mountains. Tom killed them and brought in their heads as proof. The grizzly trophies were eagerly received and kept for display purposes, but the reward money was slower in being produced. Tobin also had brought in a diary which he found in Vivian's pocket. In the diary twenty-two murders by the Espinosas had been noted, beginning in the San Luis Valley, moving through their trip to the north, and then again in the San Luis area. Although the diary later disappeared, it confirmed the deeds which could be ascribed to this pair of bedeviled souls.

The following summer South Park was the theater of action of yet another outlaw band, Jim Reynolds and his gang. Reynolds had been in the park before, working a placer at Fairplay in 1860. In 1861 he and his brother John were arrested in Denver as Confederates. However, the jailer was a Southern sympathizer and let them go. Although reports are conflicting, the Reynolds brothers apparently went to Texas and joined Rebel guerrilla forces there. Their band then robbed a wagon train of about $40,000 and headed for Colorado.

After burying the money near Pueblo, they moved on into South Park where they intended to seize a fortune from the mines for the Southern cause. Heading north through South Park, some of them stopped overnight on July 25 at Adolf Guiraud's ranch. Guiraud and Reynolds apparently had been acquainted in former years. That night Reynolds wrote a number of letters and asked Guiraud when McClelland's stage from Buckskin would reach McLaughlin's Ranch as he wanted his letters to go out on that coach. (McLaughlin's Ranch was a stage station near Hamilton and the later site of Como. It had been Stubb's Ranch earlier and would belong to George Lechner in the 1870's when he opened up the coal mines there. The fellow who was running the station in 1864 was Dan McLaughlin, not Matthew McLaughlin who owned the stage line at Fairplay.)

On the morning of July 26 the stage at Buckskin was loaded. In the express was about $1,000 which Father Dyer had just delivered with the mail from Breckenridge. Also, in the strong box was a sizable amount of gold from the new Orphan Boy mine. The mail contained additional currency and checks. No passengers were riding that day—only the driver and McClelland.

Before the coach reached McLaughlin's, the Reynolds Gang arrived and tied up the proprietor and a Major H. H. DeMary from California Gulch who was waiting for a coach. When the

117

stage arrived, the outlaws took over. They took a watch and cash from McClelland and then broke into the strong box from which they got about $3,000, although some versions of the adventure push the estimate much higher. The bandits also rifled the mail for currency and checks.

The sequence of events which followed the stage holdup is not entirely clear. During the next few days some ranches and the Michigan House stage station were robbed while the guerrillas used the region of the park between Kenosha Hill and Georgia Pass as their rendezvous and hideout. The express at Hamilton was safe, though. William Berry had just brought it in from Fairplay when news of the robbery at McLaughlin's reached him. Berry put the gold dust which he was carrying in the safest place of which he knew—under the manure in a stable, a solution which he would use again in later years under different circumstances.

Until August 4 no stage passengers were permitted to leave Denver for South Park because of the guerrilla trouble, the *Rocky Mountain News* reported. By that date the band had been ambushed in Hall's Valley across Kenosha Pass. When they were discovered, the men were dividing up some of the gold dust. The rest of the loot already had been buried in cans and has never been recovered. In the skirmish the posse killed one of the outlaws and took his head back to Montgomery to display as a trophy.

In their escape some of the guerrillas went down across South Park and stopped to eat and sleep at Guiraud's ranch, which had been deserted. The next day a large posse under the leadership of Lieutenant Shoup picked up their trail and pursued them south toward Canon City. One of the gang was captured south of Currant Creek Pass and taken to Fairplay where his life was spared in return for his revealing where the others were. The hero who made this capture was Hugh Murdock, the landlord of the South Park Hotel at Fairplay.

On the basis of the information learned from the prisoner, Jim Reynolds and four others of the gang were captured in camp near Canon City and taken to Denver. It was decided that these five were to be taken secretly to Fort Lyons for trial. About thirty miles southeast of Denver, the wagon carrying the prisoners was halted by its guards so as to water the animals. While the mounted cavalry escorting them moved on ahead of them, the guerrillas all were shot and killed. Responsible citizens protested what had happened, insisting that high authorities in Denver had planned the outcome in advance. In his own account Father Dyer swore that he personally had observed the loading of the prisoners at Denver and one of the guards was the very stage driver who had been held up at McLaughlin's.

In the meantime John Reynolds and two others had managed to make their escape to New Mexico. Knowing that the outlaws were headed through the Huerfano Butte country south of Pueblo, the residents there were notified by Shoup to arrest any men if they stopped there. Two of the band did go into a store for supplies but were permitted to go on.

Lieutenant Shoup's indignation, first roused by the merciless slaying of his brother by the Espinosas, had been fanned into a fanatical righteousness during the second summer of crime in South Park, especially since political loyalties had become involved. He arrested all of the men in the settlement at Huerfano Butte and took them to the county seat at Buckskin Joe to be tried for aiding Confederates. The jury of miners acquitted them, and so the episode of the Reynolds Gang was closed.

However, one cannot resist conjecturing about the forces that were shaping the character of the settlements in South Park. Were some of the Buckskin Greys on the jury that heard the trial of the Mexican folk from the Huerfano country? Or did the rough, raw miners at the "liveliest little burg in South Park" simply have their own code of ethics which, differing from Fairplay's, included mercy?

CHAPTER SEVEN

Mining: 1871 to the Present

The historian Frederick Jackson Turner said that the gold rushes in North America ended forever the difference between Indian country and the "civilized" Eastern Seaboard. In South Park the mining boom of the 1860's did end the era of the Indians. A vacuum followed the first wave of gold mining. The 1870's did not bring about a re-establishment of the Indian, of course, but instead a second wave of miners and the establishment of some permanent settlements.

In this second wave, silver was king. Silver had consistently appeared mixed with the gold panned and mined in South Fork in the 1860's. But not until 1871 were rich deposits found in large quantities there.

MT. BROSS AND ALMA

Although silver mining had begun in Georgetown in the previous decade, the first good silver mine in Colorado was the Moose Mine high on Mt. Bross. The discovery, made by Captain Plummer in 1871, was located at 13,860 feet.

The Moose was worked that first winter by its owners—Plummer, J. H. Dudley, and a Mr. Myers—possibly of Montgomery. The following summer, 1872, the area was thronging with down-on-their luck prospectors, while the Moose ownership was transferred to Dudley, A. W. Gill, and a McNab. In the five years that followed the discovery of the Moose, other rich deposits of ore were located on Mt. Bross and Mt. Lincoln—the Dolly Varden in 1872, the Russia, the Hiawatha, and the Australia being the best. The Australia was within 300 feet of the top of 14,284-foot Mt. Lincoln. The Present Help was higher at 14,200 feet.

Quartzville was revived in 1871 or 1872 as a camp of cabins and tents for men working in the cluster of mines above. By 1873 its population had reached about 200 and soon warranted a post office and a bank. Sometime in the 1880's the place was abandoned, although the Quartzville Tunnel was dug as late as 1884 in a disappointing attempt to reach ore.

Another short-lived camp, Hillsdale, was built north of Quartzville Gulch on the west side of the South Platte River. Located at about 11,000 feet, Hillsdale provided timbers for the mines. This lumber camp had a population of only a couple of dozen. It was in existence from 1871 until sometime in the 1880's with a post office.

Headquarters for the Moose Mining Company were established at the town of Dudley in 1871. A post office was located there in that year. Dudley, or Dudleyville as it was occasionally called, was named for Judson H. Dudley, the principal owner of the Moose. The town was a mile above the present village of Alma on the old road to Montgomery at Sawmill Creek. By 1872 it possessed stores, a livery stable, two saloons, and a boarding-house, as well as the mining company's assay and business offices and sampling works.

In 1872 E. D. Peters built a smelter at Dudley between the old road and the Platte River. The mill, evidently one owned by the Moose Company, handled ore from all of the nearby silver mines. In 1873 Peters made changes in the smelter's lead process, converting it to a copper reverboratory type. However, the copper matte produced then had to be sent to Germany for further treatment and, thus, the works never operated at a profit. The Peters smelter closed in 1875.

Dudley's population was 150 in 1874 and 100 in 1877. It had a hotel—the Dudley; mining company headquarters for the Moose, Horseshoe, and Lincoln mines; and the Mt. Lincoln Smelting Works. A cemetery was located on the ridge between the Platte River and the old road.

By 1877 J. H. Dudley had disposed of his stock in the Moose,

121

his shares being sold for about $80,000. At the time only eight men were working the mine. The town was nearly deserted after 1880 and post office service ceased. And by 1890 the Moose Mine, which had yielded a total of about $3,000,000, had almost completely shut down. A geological survey report accounted for its failure, giving as reasons the problems in early management, excessive drain on profits after the company was owned in New York, and the high cost of expensive but inadequate smelting equipment.

During these years Montgomery briefly raised its head again, because of the activity on Mt. Bross and Mt. Lincoln. One of the prospectors there was "Commodore Stephen Decatur," brother of Illinois' Governor Bross. Decatur prospected high on Mt. Lincoln in 1871, the echoes of Bross's pious hymn accompanied by the clang of the pick and shovel of the family's black sheep. (Decatur had a habit of leaving wives and families here and there.)

In the meantime, Professor DuBois was in and around Montgomery, where he was experimenting with new types of furnaces for refining silver and was purchasing ore for treatment. Although several of the old houses at Montgomery were moved away at this time to Quartzville and Alma, the town continued to survive. In 1877 the fifteen-stamp Pioneer Mill and the Piqua Ore Dressing Works both were operating. The town still appeared on a map of 1891.

Montgomery was to experience another revival around 1898, when an electric tramway was proposed for the mines above town; but it died once and for all in the 1900's. In 1954 the City of Colorado Springs built Montgomery Dam at the location to store water from its Blue River diversion project. Construction crews found several buildings still standing, including the Magnolia ore mill which was left intact above the falls.

In the early months of 1873 the town of Alma was established at the junction of Buckskin Creek and the South Platte River. Like Fairplay just seven miles down the Platte, Alma was to become a permanent town. It was named for Alma Janes, the popular daughter of a local storekeeper. The first houses belonged to

J. B. Stansell, who formerly was prominent in Buckskin Joe, and Abraham Bergh, later prominent in Fairplay.

The location of the town was strategic, for it was accessible to the silver districts that were to develop above town, especially on Mt. Bross but also in the gulches of Mosquito and Buckskin creeks. In 1873 the Boston and Colorado Smelting Company of Blackhawk opened a branch works in Alma. Associated in this enterprise were Professor N. P. Hill, who had developed the Blackhawk plant and its process, Henry R. Wolcott, Herman Berger, and Hill's metallurgist Professor Richard Pearce. Pearce ran the Alma furnace operating on his Swansea (Wales) process. Augustus R. Meyer's smelter later was built in town also. These smelting works, together with those at Dudley and another erected three miles downstream at Holland in 1874, made Alma the refining center for the region.

(The Holland smelter was organized by Dwight G. and Park Holland as the Chicago and New York Mining and Smelting Company. It treated principally the iron, copper, gold, and silver ores taken from nearby Gravel Hill. The town was still in existence with a post office in 1884, apparently having grown some after 1880 when it had no post office. However, the works lacked the necessary galena for reducing ores and was never a great success. Another nearby town of the early 1880's was Cottage Grove between Alma and Holland.)

The smelters made it possible for the mine operators to dispose of their ore in the immediate neighborhood, whereas some of the ore previously was even shipped to Wales. The South Park Pool Association was organized by Hill, Wolcott, Berger, Pearce, Stansell, and others, in the pattern of later agricultural co-ops. Stansell built a large log ore bin at Alma to store the material for refining. Although silver sometimes was separated in stamp mills, most ores had to be roasted. Thus, the mines were dependent on these expensively built and operated plants. In smelting, the silver was melted and then separated by chemical processes.

The mills used expensive equipment and specialized labor. Consequently, the smelters eventually found it more economical to centralize their operations. Agents bought ores in the mining districts and shipped the ore to their smelters. In 1875 some of the area's ores were purchased and shipped for the first time to Golden, where the Moore Mining and Smelting Company was operating with a simpler smelting process than most. After the Denver, South Park and Pacific Railway was built, most of South Park's silver ores were taken to Denver to the Boston and Colorado Company's new Argo Smelter.

The national economic Panic of 1873 did not greatly curtail activity in the area. In fact, the depressions elsewhere frequently brought a wave of the unemployed into the mining districts. Alma, in its first years, was a hive of activity—much of it lawless. When the English woman Isabella Bird visited the region, although not the town itself, in 1873, she reported that Alma was so lawless that vigilance committees had been organized.

By 1874 the population was 150 and in 1877 it was 700. James Moynahan, who moved into Alma from Buckskin in 1873, opened a hotel and then in 1874 a mercantile business. He later had additional stores in Fairplay and Leadville. In his long career in South Park, Moynahan was a county commissioner (1869 and 1870), mayor of Alma (1874), and a state senator (1876). He later was President *pro tem* of the Colorado State Senate and was once a candidate for nomination for governor. He owned the big Orphan Boy gold mine and in later years became a South Park rancher, raising cattle and horses.

In 1875 Alma had a weekly newspaper, the *Mount Lincoln News*, edited by W. F. Hogan. However, Hogan took his press to Leadville in 1878 with the beginning of mining excitement there. Alma's newspapers in other years were the Park County *Bulletin* (1880-1914), the Park County *Miner* (1887-1888) and the Alma *Mining Record* (1935-1936). All three were weeklies.

In 1878 Alma had Catholic, Methodist, and Presbyterian churches, as well as two saloons and three hotels. And, with the surge of traffic to Leadville, there were seven stages.

Editor Hogan was not the only one who deserted Alma for Leadville. A mass exodus soon took place. In January, 1879, only one-fourth of Alma's buildings had occupants, although the same fickle population had returned by the end of the year. A comparison of the yield of silver mines in each area explains the initial wave of enthusiasm about Leadville. Whereas the Moose had produced $900,000 in its first year in 1871, and the Dolly Varden $340,000 in 1872, Leadville's Little Pittsburgh produced $3,800,-000 in 1878 alone. With the discovery of the Fanny Barrett group of mines on Buckskin Mountain in 1879, the migrants swept back to the east side of the range to protect their own claims in the hope of another Leadville.

The general increase in mining interest continued, with a good share of the activity being in the old gold mines and placers, Alma's population reaching 900 in 1884. The Alma Placer Company had hydraulic operations working on the Platte below town. There was a bank, the Bank of Alma; a photographer; twenty-nine business houses; five saloons; and four hotels, including the famous Inter-Ocean, the Capital Hill, the St. Nicholas, and the Springs—the last two built in the seventies.

The bank was first opened by an Englishman, E. P. Arthur, and C. G. Hathaway, who also opened one in Fairplay. Joseph H. (Harry) Singleton bought the Alma bank in 1897 and the other in 1898. A Canadian, Singleton had come to Alma in 1880, in charge of a freighting concern. After two years during which he managed Moynahan's store in Fairplay, he returned to Alma and opened his own store. This he sold out to Moynahan when in 1888 he became cashier of the Bank of Alma. Harry had two sons, Jack and Fred. When Harry died in 1914, Jack took over the Fairplay bank while Fred ran the one in Alma.

The Bank of Alma was held up one day in the 1930's just as Fred was about to lock up for lunch. With customers shouting "They're robbing the bank!" and guns blazing, the two robbers made their getaway toward Hoosier Pass. However, they were caught in Indiana, ironically, and finally came to rest in the penitentiary at Canon City.

After Fred's death and the Alma fire of 1937, the bank there was consolidated with the Bank of Fairplay. The old structure from Alma now has been moved to South Park City in Fairplay.

Following the Panic of 1893 Alma's population dropped to

300 and its smelter lay idle. But when Davis Waite, Populist governor and candidate for re-election advocating free silver purchase, held a rally in Alma in 1894, the whole district was there to hear him. The issue was bimetalism, and the miners had rallied to the Populists' Presidential candidate, Bryan, the crusader against the "Cross of Gold."

The Bryan Silver Club of Fairplay came to the Alma rally *en masse,* as the late Alice Wonder recalled. Alma that day was the "noisiest, wildest" place she ever saw. McLaughlin's Concord stage and every buggy available had been hired for the occasion. On the way back to Fairplay, between Alma and nearby London Junction, a coach with thirty-five people piled onto it and into it left its running gears. The coach overturned and many were seriously injured.

Although Alma in 1882 had acquired a steam fire engine—the occasion being celebrated with a parade, ball, and supper—neither the fire department nor all the volunteers from the mines and Fairplay were able to save the town twenty-five years later. A fire at that time took out many business houses, including the post office. Most of the rest of the town burned in 1937, although the bank was saved, as was a hardware housing 500 pounds of dynamite. The fire started in a pool hall in the small hours of the morning. The river was frozen, preventing fire equipment from operating quickly, while a high wind fanned the flames.

The industry which had kept Alma alive that long was not silver but gold. In 1902 the Snowstorm Hydraulic Company had acquired the old Alma Placer below town. In addition to this location, the Snowstorm Placer as it was called, the company bought up almost all of the old placer claims upstream to Montgomery and downstream toward Fairplay. They also built a large network of ditches from the Platte River and from Buckskin, Mosquito, and Beaver creeks leading into one canal for hydraulic operations. The center of the workings came to be about half way between Alma and Fairplay. Here, with two seven-inch nozzles and one six-incher, water tore down the banks and opened large pits. Sand and gravel thus freed were washed through sluices a yard wide.

Another revival of gold mining took place in the 1930's. However, the fire of 1937, coupled with abandonment of the nearby branch railroad in the same year, sent the town rapidly downhill. Today it is a sleepy little village.

Through the late 1860's and 1870's the old Buckskin district west of Alma was never quite deserted. In fact, the 1879 discoveries around Buckskin and Loveland mountains brought 500 men into the gulch again. The town site of Buckskin Joe was pre-empted and a new town sprang up—only to die two years later.

The mines of this period were high on the mountains above timberline. The buildings of some of these mines, such as the Paris Mine on Mt. Bross, those opposite the Paris on Loveland Mountain, and the Kentucky Belle above Kite Lake still dangle over Buckskin Gulch. Clason's Map of 1911 also shows a site called Timberline Town northwest of Alma. Some of the mines have been reopened in the 1960's; and, in addition, serpentine marble is being quarried on Mt. Bross.

THE MOSQUITO DISTRICT

Mining had continued even more actively in Mosquito Gulch. In 1874 the London Mine opened, becoming an important producer of gold, silver, and lead by 1880. The London Company's ore was being reduced at Tenant's Stamp Mill in Mosquito Gulch at least by 1877. The mill and ore bins were several hundred feet below the mine, which was on the north side of London Hill at that time. For a few years power for the mill was supplied by an enormous windmill with sixty-foot arms. The windmill blew down in a storm in 1880, when a telegraph line which had been strung across Mosquito Pass to Leadville also was knocked down.

In 1882 a branch of the Denver and South Park railroad was built to the upper end of Mosquito Gulch. In that same year the London Mine built an aerial tramway, the first in Colorado, from the main entrance of the old North Mine to the mill below at the end of the railroad branch. After 1882, however, the South London Mine was the chief producer with the big mill at the latter mine being built in 1883. W. K. Jewett of Colorado Springs, who owned the mine in the late 1890's, had a tunnel bored to connect the North and South mines. The South Mine was worked as late as 1943.

The road past the London Mine was the main highway to Leadville by 1879 and became known to hundreds of travelers. That this rugged route was so popular is explained only by the fact that the distance from Fairplay to Leadville over Mosquito Pass was only twenty-one miles, whereas it was forty via Weston Pass and seventy-two by way of Trout Creek.

By the fall of 1878 a group of Leadville, Fairplay, and Denver men, including H. A. W. Tabor, incorporated the Mosquito Pass Wagon Road Company. The road was completed in the spring of 1879, construction being carried on right through the winter. The route was located in the north side of London Hill so as to avoid the marshy land in the saddle behind the mountain, although the original trail had gone around the south side of the hill. The Park County commissioners were asked to provide funds for improvement of the ten-mile approach already in existence, but they refused.

Stages from Denver stopped at Fairplay, where meals and lodging were available for three dollars. Spotswood and McClelland hayburners carried as many as fifty passengers a day each way over the pass. Other stage companies using the route were Wall and Witter's, McLaughlin's, and the "Despatch" Company's. Wall and Witter, who bought out Spotswood and McClelland in the fall of '79, maintained 400 horses and mules, seven coaches, and ten freight wagons.

A stage station called Half-Way House was located somewhere between Park City and the hairpin turn at the north end of Mosquito Gulch. This famous spot, operated by John Nugent (about whom more in a later chapter), served dinners for fifty cents. There were also a saloon, stables, and a store.

Half-Way House was destroyed by a snowslide in 1890, an act of God if ever one took place. In the years after the Leadville rush, Half-Way House became a gambling house and a brothel and was once referred to as the "Club House," an " 'inflamed joint' that sapped the existence from the miners."

Fairplay in the 1870's had become established as the commercial center for the north end of the park, as can be seen by the number of business houses on Front Street. *Courtesy of the Denver Public Library, Western Collection.*

The stone brewery, which now houses South Park City's museum, was built after a fire destroyed the old town of Fairplay, including the original brewery, in 1873.

This stone tavern was owned by Charles and Leonard Sumner, who also were the local brewers.

The county jail was built of stone, as were many of Fairplay's buildings after the 1873 fire.

This log building, which survived the big fire, was moved to Fairplay from Montgomery in 1867 by Father Dyer for use as a church. In Montgomery it was a hotel.

The Presbyterians of Fairplay built this lovely little gem of gothic architecture in 1874. Its name, Sheldon Jackson Memorial Chapel, honors the church superintendent who organized the congregation and guided the building of the chapel. *Courtesy of the Denver Public Library Western Collection, Otto Roach photo.*

The flag proudly waves over Park County's new courthouse in 1874. Its history was still unblemished by the Hanging Court's lynching. *Courtesy of the Library, State Historical Society of Colorado.*

The older portion of F a i r p l a y's schoolhouse was built in 1880.

South Park City's replica of a *tong* house is actually an old cabin brought down from Leavick. However, it nicely serves as a reminder of the club house where Fairplay's Chinese miners once met and where they received their work assignments. *Courtesy of the South Park City collection.*

134

Chinese miners worked in the placers around Fairplay from the middle 1870's until the end of the century. This view would appear to be on Beaver Creek. *Courtesy of the Library, State Historical Society of Colorado.*

Miles of ditches and canals diverted water from the Middle Fork of the South Platte as well as its tributaries to operate the huge hoses and nozzles that cut away banks for hydraulic mining, at Alma in this instance. *Courtesy of the Library, State Historical Society of Colorado, T. C. Miller photo.*

This view of the Alma Placer shows the extent to which the earth was torn up by the hydraulic method of making molehills out of mountains. *Courtesy of the Denver Public Library Western Collection.*

What the hydraulic hoses left unfinished, the dredges undertook to accomplish. This gold dredge, with Mt. Bross in the background, is on Beaver Creek near Alma. *Courtesy of the South Park City collection.*

The wreckage of an abandoned "gold boat" at Fairplay. *Courtesy of the Denver Public Library Western Collection.*

138

During the 1930's and into the 1950's a new, larger dredge worked on the South Platte below Fairplay. Floating in a lake which it created as it progressed, the dredge chewed up the streambed at one end and spewed out tailings from the other. Ores were partially treated in the dredge. *U. S. Geological Survey, L. C. Huff photo.*

139

Buckets on the Fairplay dredge. *U. S. Geological Survey, L. C. Huff photo.*

Fairplay's Front Street in the early 1900's. *Courtesy, South Park City collection.*

Entrance to the South Park City restoration which has brought together old buildings from ghost towns around the park to recreate an old-time mining town. *Courtesy, South Park City collection.*

141

The cluster of buildings beyond Lake Como is King where coal was mined extensively in the 1880's and 1890's. A short branch line ran from the Denver and South Park to King. Although indistinct, this picture is the only one known to exist of the town. The reproduction is a greatly enlarged portion of a panorama taken by William H. Jackson, and the town was spotted in the original plate quite by accident. *Courtesy of the Library, State Historical Society of Colorado.*

A seldom-heard-of ghost town in South Park is Balfour, near Currant Creek Pass. Lasting for only five years or so, it was a latter-day gold mining camp, established in 1894. The town was only ten days old when this photograph was made. *Courtesy of the Denver Public Library Western Collection, Carnahan photo.*

The bleak, deserted site of Balfour in the south end of the park, in 1965.

In 1880, with the completion of the railroad to Leadville, the Mosquito toll road was passé, and the toll road company went out of business in 1882. Travelers were glad to abandon the jarring, dusty trip. Despite legends about bandits on Mosquito Pass, the route had been comparatively safe in that respect. Only one stage robbery is known to have occurred on the road, and that was close to Leadville.

Throughout this period the rich Orphan Boy mine, opened in the early 1860's, had continued to be worked in lower Mosquito Gulch. The Hock-Hocking Mine, a silver producer, was located in 1879 opposite the Orphan Boy; it was worked until 1900 and again in the mid-1900's. The Orphan Boy operated into the 1900's. A Sterling City Mining Company was also still operating in the 1880's.

With the combined activity from the Leadville road and the local mines in the gulch, Park City sprang up in 1879 only 300 feet from the Orphan Boy. Undoubtedly, there had been a camp near the mine for its workers in the years before. (A letter dated April 19, 1859, mentions that a town in South Park had been started and was called Park City, but it is impossible to conjecture whether this place was at the same site or elsewhere.)

In 1879 Park City had about 200 people and a dozen or two business houses, four hotels, and a post office, but even the arrival of the Denver and South Park in 1882 did not help much to stop the drift away from the town which had begun after the Mosquito Pass road fell into disuse. The neighboring mines kept a handful of people there for a number of years; and several houses, some still occupied, remain at the town today.

The rest of the gulch above Park City has been abandoned to the winds and snows of Mosquito Pass. Weather has destroyed many of the old buildings, although a few remain at the London Mines. When a telephone line was run across the pass in 1889, it came down the next spring, the same year in which Loveland Mountain's snowslides claimed Half-Way House. Telephone poles were placed closer and closer together until only seventeen feet apart in an effort to keep the lines up, but eventually the problem was solved by burying them.

For a few years a town called Mahoneyville also existed in the vicinity of London Hill, and in 1899 snowslides which again took out the long distance telephone lines and the London Mine lines were also reported at a place by that name.

In 1937 Leadville was urging reconstruction of the Mosquito Pass road against the opposition of Park County. It now has been improved enough to be used by stout-hearted drivers of automobiles. In recent years the route around the south side of London Hill has become the scene of an annual burro race from Leadville to Fairplay. Burros carry a 25-pound pack while their owners walk, run, push, or carry them but are not permitted to ride them. Best time for the race is a little over three hours.

THE SACRAMENTO, HORSESHOE, AND WESTON DISTRICTS

South of the Mosquito District the Leadville boom of 1878 stimulated ore discoveries at locations which had not been mined in the 1860's. In the late 1870's there sprang up several little mining camps, all of which now are ghost towns or have totally disappeared. These camps were sprinkled along the mountains from Mt. Sherman south to Horseshoe Mountain. Since considerable confusion exists about their names and locations, an attempt —though perhaps faulty—will be made to locate them in time and place.

In October, 1878, pockets of silver were discovered in Little Sacramento Gulch about six miles west of Fairplay by Dwelle, Tobie, Mullen, LeDuc, and Birdzell. These men together formed the Sacramento Mining Company and drove the October Tunnel, later called the Lark Tunnel. As other claims were discovered, pock-marking the cliffs on the south side of the gulch, the original ones remained the center of activity. A smelter, located at the mouth of the gulch, served the mines. (This smelter may have been at a town called Condon which appears on a map of 1880 about three miles north and west of Fairplay.)

The Sacramento Mine was worked extensively until 1883, when English investors bought it. Dwelle was active in the company even until 1895. Its rich lodes of ore were worked at times by as many as sixty men. Often the walls of the pockets of ore were lined with glittering encrustations of mineral.

The town—variously called Sacramento City or Flats—had about twenty cabins. Some still stand today, reinforced with rock to the roofs as protection against wind and snow. The mining office has collapsed. Recently some efforts have been made to reopen the mine and to build a mill and smelter at the bottom of Sacramento Gulch to give impetus to new mining interests throughout the region.

The Forest Reserve Map of 1898 shows the town of East Leadville about a mile southeast of Sacramento. It has been said that East Leadville was another name for Sacramento; however, not only do both places appear on that map but also both are listed separately in a postal directory as early as 1880. (Each town got its mail from Fairplay.) East Leadville also is said to have been another name for the town of Horseshoe, but the same postal directory for 1880 lists Horseshoe as a post office in its own right.

The Fairplay *Flume* of May 29, 1879, said that a plat of the town of East Leadville had been recorded by J. H. B. McFerran to be built in Horseshoe Gulch, ten miles east of Leadville. McFerran, of Colorado Springs, was working the Last Chance Mine on Mt. Sheridan and owned a smelter in the gulch, according to the story. William Shortridge was to build a hotel at East Leadville that summer. By 1900 both Sacramento and East Leadville were nearly abandoned. A building found in the woods southeast of Sacramento in 1965 is most likely the hotel at the site of East Leadville.

McFerran's smelter, the South Park Smelting and Reduction Works, was listed in the Colorado Directory of Mines for 1879. It was at Eureka, five miles below the mine on Mt. Sheridan. Such a description might put Eureka about a mile east of the site of Horseshoe, not down on the creek but somewhere along the old abandoned road to Fairplay. The smelter was being worked by forty men in 1879 and could handle about ten tons of ore a day.

On Fourmile Creek, formerly called simply Horseshoe Gulch, were the towns of Leavick, New or West Leavick, Horseshoe, and Mudsill. Horseshoe was laid out in 1878. It was coming into its own in 1880, when it had a post office, two hotels—the Leadville and the Palmer—and a population of seventy-five. By the next year it had a summer population of 800, although only 300 year round, according to one set of figures; but this number may have been for the entire gulch as the town itself polled only forty-three votes in an election to incorporate the town in 1881.

By 1884 the Hanlin family was much in evidence—M. R. Hanlin being postmaster, George Hanlin running the Hanlin House, and the two owning the Hanlin Brothers General Merchandise store. Considerable lumbering was done for the mines above timberline. Horseshoe never recovered after the Panic of 1893 and was not shown on the 1898 Forest Reserve map. By 1940 only two cabins were said to remain, and even those are gone today.

Mudsill, the railroad station for Horseshoe, was built in 1892 when a branch of the Colorado and Southern came up the gulch (see Chapter VIII). It was still on maps in 1917. Apparently the station came to be called Horseshoe after a while, and the former town of Horseshoe was called "Old Town." Therefore, it is quite possible that what most people have called the site of Horseshoe is really the site of Mudsill, which was about a mile above the original site of Horseshoe.

The Mudsill Mine was located on the north rim of the Horseshoe cirque. The mine was originally opened in 1880 and reputedly was salted and sold to the Lord Mayor of London for $190,000. Not long before that "Chicken Bill" of Leadville had salted it for another customer who did not bite. The Mudsill group, occuping 260 acres, was sold in 1938 for only $20,000.

In 1873 Samuel MacMillan had discovered an outcrop of silver near the head of Horseshoe Gulch. The location of this was in the Mt. Sheridan-Peerless Mountain section where several of the best mines were found later. In 1887 the Hilltop Mine was opened at about 13,000 feet on Mt. Sheridan. In this mine was a glittering chamber lined with mineral and called the Ice Palace. In addition to silver, rich lead and zinc ores have been taken from the Hilltop. The Dauntless Mine was opened below the

148

Hilltop and a little south of it, and a tunnel was driven back in toward the Hilltop.

In 1892 Felix Leavick of Leadville bought out the Hilltop Mine, but within a year the Panic brought its operation to a standstill. In 1895 it reopened and the following year the Denver, South Park, and Hilltop Railroad was built to the mill, which had been treating the ores from the Hilltop and neighboring mines. The mill was at the fork of Fourmile Creek below Peerless Mountain. An aerial tram brought ore from the Hilltop town to the mill. Now, in 1896, the place finally got a name, Leavick, and in 1897 a post office. The name of the post office was changed from Leavick to Doran in 1902, however.

Alice Wonder described Leavick as it was in 1899 when she taught a short session of school there. (Several of the camps held these "short sessions" of a few weeks' length, not because the miners cared a great deal about education but because their children would not be entitled to any school in the camp at all if this minimal gesture were not made each year.) The town was built in the gulch with only one street, according to her report. The town had a store with its post office, a cook house, a few cabins, and the small frame schoolhouse up the street. Several men were batching in one house.

However, many of the miners lived farther up the gulch closer to the mines. This other cluster of cabins was called West Leavick or New Leavick, but it was not a town as such.

The Hilltop and the Last Chance proved to be the rich producers, but both alternated between years of operation and inactivity. There was a flurry in 1907 and another around 1920. The railroad was dismantled in 1937, but a few men were still working the Hilltop in the 1940's, living in the old boardinghouse there. There was at one time talk of tunneling through the Ice Palace to take ore out on the Leadville side of the mountain, and today the tunnel from the Dauntless is being pushed toward the Hilltop again. The boardinghouse has collapsed and the few remaining buildings of Leavick down in the gulch have been taken to South Park City in Fairplay.

During the 1870's and 1880's the Mosquito Range was occasionally crossed on foot via Horseshoe Pass. Father Dyer used it in 1874 when he went to visit his son Elias. He dropped down over the mountains into Iowa Gulch, his description of the route taken placing the pass between the Hilltop Mine and the summit of Mount Sheridan. (Elias Dyer had a mine in Iowa Gulch, the Dyer Mine. After Elias' murder in 1875, Father Dyer sold his half interest in the mine for $3,000 to H. A. W. Tabor; and Tabor, of course, sold it for $60,000 two years later.)

The next crossing of the Mosquito Range south of Horseshoe was the heavily used Weston Pass. Little mining was done south of the Horseshoe district, but Weston Pass did have two fair-sized silver mines—the Weston and the Danser—as well as a few smaller ones. The mines were opened in 1883, worked a short time and a little again in 1901. Much of the ore taken out was left in bins at the top of the pass.

Weston Pass's fame in the mining era rests, instead, in its use for passenger and freight traffic to and from Leadville in the short period between 1878 and 1880. At a mere 11,945 feet, it was easier, though longer, than the Mosquito Pass route out of Fairplay. However, it was quite direct for traffic from Colorado Springs. Jim McGee hauled 100 tons of freight a day from Colorado Springs over Weston Pass to Leadville at the peak. Later in the 1880's McLaughlin ran freight and coaches over the pass but at a loss.

(The route from Colorado Springs and Colorado City to South Park and Leadville still was through Ute Pass and west to Wilkerson Pass, a road which was used heavily not only during the Leadville rush but also in the mid-1870's after the San Juan region opened up. At that time large freighting trains crossed the park and then rumbled on down Trout Creek Pass to reach the southwestern part of the state. Otherwise, Wilkerson Pass was not a part of the great mining excitement in South Park. Its only mining was a zinc and lead body which was worked in 1874. Called the Great Western, the mine was at the top of the 9,525-foot high pass.)

At the eastern end of Weston Pass was Rich Stage Station. which, like other stage stations, served also as a polling place

150

during elections. Once during the 1870's mules were registered as voters at Rich Station in an all-out effort to defeat an unpopular banker from Fairplay.

Platte Station was a more prominent, and somewhat more permanent, location. It existed as a post office from 1880 until at least 1884 and still appeared on a map as late as 1891. It had a population of fifty in 1884, although most of the people were engaged in ranching after the railroad to Leadville took over the freighting business in 1880. Platte Station was fourteen miles west of Garo and fourteen miles south of Fairplay, the principal supply town and transportation center at the north end of the park.

FAIRPLAY

Fairplay had long since settled into being a permanent—if raw—frontier town with a population that usually numbered three or four hundred and with enough variety in its economic life to keep it going. It served freight and passenger traffic coming or going across the park on the Denver route, but it also had become the established trading center for all of the mining and ranching districts that ringed Fairplay. Furthermore, it was secure in its role as the county seat of Park County.

In the early 1870's Fairplay was served by a dozen or more stage runs. Three came in weekly from Denver on the Colorado Stage Company line which continued on to Santa Fe. Coaches came in three times a week from Colorado Springs, and twice a week from San Luis "Park" and Lake County on Frank Logan's line. W. H. Berry, who had been in the express business during the Reynolds Gang affair, ran one stage a week to Canon City. And once a week a coach ran across Hoosier Pass. Spotswood and McClelland had the South Park Stage Company, which was not only the longest line but also owner of the best equipment and service. Wells Fargo and Company had an express office in Fairplay which served all of South Park with the exception of the upper Tarryall, for which Hamilton still maintained an office.

151

McLaughlin and Hall kept a large livery stable at Fairplay for the great number of animals relayed in traffic.

For the travelers Fairplay also provided two hotels, Hugh Murdock's South Park House and Miller's Clinton House. Although the more celebrated of the two, the South Park House set a table that left much to be desired in both cuisine and atmosphere. Tourists with camping outfits still preferred to set up tents outside of town, as had the Colfax party. The handful of businesses, including A. M. Janes' general store and Valiton's drugstore, provided their immediate needs.

A. M. Janes, who also was Fairplay's postmaster, ran his store in the same building where William H. Berry had his express and stage office. Berry bore a chipped shoulder about his neighbor next door, because he wanted the contract for carrying gold out of Oro City by express, but Oro's postmaster, H. A. W. Tabor, persisted in sending dust and nuggets with the regular mail dispatches.

In 1869 two bags of gold as well as some letters had been stolen by a fellow named Farnum, one of the carriers between Oro City and Fairplay. When a posse had searched his stable in Fairplay, they had found the stolen items under some manure. Although Farnum seemed to think that the gold should be his as payment of back wages, he was, nevertheless, found guilty of embezzling and stealing from the mails. In 1872 the ruling was reversed on the grounds that gold was not classed as mailable matter.

In the meantime, Tabor, as was still his custom despite the Farnum episode, put in the mail for Denver a buckskin bag containing a thousand dollars' worth of gold. The money was wrapped in newsprint, and a letter with forty dollars enclosed was placed in the bag also. The package arrived safely in Fairplay, where Janes received it, Berry being in the store at the time. Janes stashed the bag away to await the morning dispatch to Denver.

That night Berry got together a dance on the spur of the moment. Janes and his store clerk both were there. Although Berry forgot some of the refreshments and had to leave for a while to get them, the party was a great success. The next morning

152

when Janes went to put up the mail, he discovered that the bag of nuggets and dust was gone. Berry pitched in and searched the cellar for Janes, finding there bits of newspaper identified as the one from the pouch. Beyond that discovery, the incident lay unsolved for several weeks.

However, in the fall a special agent came to Fairplay to investigate the case. After following up various leads and suspects, the agent began to believe that beneath Berry's facade of respectability, there lurked a bravado that rang untrue. Perhaps it was the too-eager sign in the window of Berry's new office offering a reward for the thief's apprehension which tipped off the agent. Or perhaps it was Berry's curly red beard that clearly meant he was a roguish type. At any rate, the alert agent went to Berry's stable and there in Fairplay's favorite hiding place for mail—under the manure—he found incriminating bits of string and paper.

Berry confessed that on the night of the dance he had squeezed through a small window into the store when he had gone out for the refreshments. He had taken the gold then and had it with him even as he aided in the search of the store in the morning. However, Berry claimed that his motive was confined to settling his grievance with Tabor, and such may have been the case—if one disregards the fact that some of the gold had been disposed of after the theft. Berry paid back the total amount; and, in view of his fine reputation (and family connections by marriage), the case was dismissed.

One traveler investigated the cemetery in 1871. He reported that there were twenty-two graves, but only three of the deaths had been natural. The Methodist Church had no preacher although $3,000 had been spent on the mission but without a soul saved, according to one report. The last preacher, in fact, had been discharged because of misconduct. However, there was a stable element in the area that sent forth forty-five offspring to school in 1871. The town proudly boasted of fifteen families and eleven "marriageable young ladies." By 1873 the local men had even petitioned for a dispensation for a Masonic Lodge.

A notable group which stopped over at Fairplay in 1873 was

the U. S. Geological Survey party under Dr. F. V. Hayden. Having surveyed the general route of the Union Pacific and the east slope of the Rockies with special interest in mineral and coal deposits in 1869, the geologists had entered South Park that year. They examined the salt springs there and Horseshoe Mountain. The latter they described as looking like a broken crater with melted material poured in regular strata over the sides. The floor of the park was one great "quaquaversal" in their words. William H. Jackson, the famous photographer with the party, reported that they climbed Mt. Lincoln and one of his best early photographs was taken there at the "famous Montezuma silver mine near the top." He also said of Fairplay that it was "not quite as wide open as Cheyenne in 1869. But we found it would serve." Jackson left Fairplay that year riding a white mule Dolly, which accompanied him for the next five years when he was with the Survey.

In 1873 they had been working in Wyoming when Indian trouble prompted them to move to Colorado. There they set up four meteorological observation sites for the field season of 1873. These were at Denver, Canon City, Fairplay, and the top of Mt. Lincoln. The Survey also continued its explorations and mappings of the mountains. The organizational plan was such that the operation was divided into three divisions, one of which headquartered in South Park under the leadership of Gannett. Each division had five to a dozen men. All three divisions and Hayden himself rendezvoused in Fairplay in July before moving into the various field assignments. The results of the Survey's labors appeared in 1877 in the invaluable *Atlas of Colorado*.

During the year 1873 almost the entire town of Fairplay burned, and after that fire the present town of Fairplay began to emerge. Even the name of the town finally became established, for it had been called South Park City after a legal change was made in 1869. McLaughlin, Murdock, and Janes were prominent as officers of the town of South Park City. In 1874 the Territorial Legislature changed the name back to Fairplay. As the new Fairplay rose from the ashes, a stone structure for the courthouse and another for the brewery were erected.

Catholics and Presbyterians alike took a renewed interest in the plight of the town. Under Father Robinson, the Catholic charge had the status of a mission to receive periodical visits.

The Presbyterians under the leadership of Sheldon Jackson built in 1874 the lacy white chapel which still stands in Fairplay. Jackson had become the superintendent of all Presbyterian missions in the West in 1869 and had moved his headquarters to Denver in 1871. He first organized a group of eight in Fairplay in 1872 and provided continuing interest in the subsequent years. (Jackson became the first ordained missionary to Alaska from the United States in 1877, was appointed Superintendent of Education in Alaska in 1885, and had the unique distinction of introducing 539 reindeer into Alaska from Norway, to round out his career.)

Richard S. Allen published the Fairplay *Sentinel* from 1875 until 1878, when it joined Alma's migrating *Mount Lincoln News* in Leadville. The Fairplay *Flume* began publication in February of 1879, appearing continuously until December 27, 1918. The *Flume* then merged with the Park County *Republican* (1912-1919) as the *Park County Republican and Fairplay Flume* until 1940. Fairplay also had its Park County *News* from 1925 until 1930.

The Leadville rush and the opening of the Sacramento-Horseshoe district increased Fairplay's importance as its population grew to 500. The Fairplay Hotel opened to give some competition to the new Bergh House which had been built in 1876 by Abraham Bergh. In 1880 the two-storied stone schoolhouse was built. By 1883 the population was 800, and Fairplay had twelve stores, a smelter, and the Bank of Fairplay—in addition to the perennial brewery and saloons; and the Methodists again had a preacher.

Fairplay developed a more stable atmosphere in the 1880's, which was an abrupt change from the brash vigor of its earlier years. The headstrong, unruly segment of its population finally had gone beyond the limits even of frontier ethics in 1879 and 1880, and a rather self-conscious, chastened calm settled on the town in the following years.

The Leadville rush had brought a great number of drifters through the park, and they left in their wake an assortment of troubles and crimes. In March, 1879, a freighter named Dingman was held up in South Park by three brazen horsemen within sight of several other wagons on the road. Countless other robberies took place that summer. However, South Park was too big an area to police, and there were so many strangers on the roads that the law made no attempt to apprehend the culprits. It was the accepted rule among travelers that they should defend themselves on the road as best they could. "Shoot on sight" was the order of the day.

Since the first days of the gold rush, the settlers had felt both a need and a justification for taking the law into their own hands. The self-constituted Jefferson Territory and the mining courts were examples of efforts in the direction of responsible self-government. But another spirit had been at work in the arbitrary moving of a county seat, the willingness—even eagerness—to pass judgments and to dole out punishments without the benefit of a legal court, and to disregard pridefully the law in many cases. There was something of this latter spirit in the righteous temper that spawned the vigilantes.

The courts in Fairplay had become unpopular with the citizens by passing a number of excessively light sentences and by acquitting individuals who appeared to be guilty of serious crimes. It was even suspected that bribery was involved. In April of 1879 Frank Jones was indicted for murder but got a sentence of only eight years in the penitentiary. In the next few months two men were freed despite charges of assault with intent to kill. In April, 1880, John Laughlin, who apparently was guilty of murder, was freed.

The incident of the Hanging Court brought the trouble to a crisis. John Hoover, a long-time resident of South Park and the owner of Fairplay's Capital Bar and Billiard Parlor, was the victim, though not an innocent one. Hoover was an irascible fellow, especially when he was drinking, and he was drinking most of the time. During the spring of 1879 a drainage ditch on the new Fairplay Hotel property had been overflowing into Hoover's yard. In response to his complaints, the hotel hired a young stage driver, Tom Bennett, to repair the ditch. Instead of getting the job finished up properly, Bennett took an afternoon off down at the Bergh House. When Hoover found his yard full of water again, he went after Bennett and put two bullets into him, killing him. Hoover gave himself up.

After waiting in jail for a year, Hoover finally was tried before Judge Thomas Bowen on April 26, 1880. He was found guilty of manslaughter rather than murder and was sentenced to only eight years in prison. The local citizens were enraged. That night a group of men wearing masks went to the home of Sheriff Efinger and demanded that Hoover be turned over to them. He refused. The mob then went to the jail, where the guards were overpowered and Hoover's cell was unlocked. The prisoner was taken from the jail to the second floor of the stone courthouse, and he was there hanged from a window over the main entrance.

When the judge entered the court on the following morning, there was a coiled rope on his desk. The judge did not wait to adjourn the court. He and the district attorney simply left town as swiftly as possible.

The Fairplay *Flume* soon carried an advertisement which read, "Citizens, our laws are a farce! Our District Attorney bought! . . . 105 men, brave and true, in this county alone have sworn to enforce the laws and punish *Murderers*. We are backed by $100,000 and several thousand men in other parts of the State! We mean business! We are carefully watching 3 persons in Fairplay who are meddling with our affairs!"

The notice went on to threaten with lynching anyone who arrested or "tampered with" those who had hanged "Hoover the murderer." It warned, "Beware of the Vigilantes!" and was signed, "Coffin."

Shortly thereafter a drunk at Alma set out to shoot the first man he met and, unfortunately, he succeeded. The "Hundred and Five" lost no time in getting to Alma to take care of the murderer, Sam Porter. They promptly strung him up.

When a new judge arrived to hold court in June, Cicero Simms was sentenced to be hanged for another murder. That time a crowd of more than a thousand gathered for the execution—just to be sure that it was done. With the hanging of Cicero Simms,

Fairplay felt that justice was assured again in the courts, and the "Hundred and Five" retired.

During these years of the 1870's and 1880's Fairplay had remained an important gold mining center in its own right. The present-day piles of dredged rubble along the South Platte testify to the many decades in which its mining continued, its changing methods a sign of "progress."

After one-man placers had become too unfruitful to be continued, larger mining companies had acquired the claims and had begun to introduce hydraulic equipment. One of the earliest of these companies in the Fairplay area belonged to Frederick Clark and J. W. Smith, who owned four miles of land and 1,000 acres of placers. Clark had come to Denver in 1860 and opened a store which burned out in 1863 and flooded out in 1864. But he struck it rich in silver at Georgetown. After observing California's gold mining methods, Clark decided to go into hydraulic gold mining.

The hydraulic process required an unlimited supply of water, for which Clark had a large system of ditches and flumes built at Fairplay. He installed the necessary and expensive equipment which made hydraulic mining prohibitive to small operators. In addition to water and patented equipment, hydraulic mining also required plenty of unskilled labor, and for this Clark turned to Edward L. Thayer.

Clark and Smith brought Thayer to Fairplay in 1875 as contractor for the labor force. Thayer brought with him some 200 Chinese workers. As a sailing merchant, Thayer had gone to China in earlier years and had been hired there by the Chinese "Six Companies" around 1860 to be an employment agent for orientals going to the United States. He had been responsible for securing jobs for many of them in California and then brought several into the Gilpin district in 1873. The Gilpin and Fairplay areas were the only two mining sections in Colorado where Chinese labor was used to any great extent.

Thayer's procedure was to lease mining land and then to sublease it to the Chinese. The Chinese were not allowed to buy land as they were not citizens of the United States. Thayer served as intermediary for the Chinese in many aspects of their daily living and, in turn, had their confidence and loyalty.

In 1876 Clark was killed when a derrick fell on him, but Thayer continued to direct the placer operation until a cloud-burst and flood in 1878 wiped out the dams, ditches, and sluices. Thayer shortly thereafter was hired by former Governor John Evans and J. W. Smith to be agent for workers at the nearby Como coal mines. Thayer was superintendent at Como until 1890 when he suffered a stroke during a trip from Como to Fairplay in a blizzard.

Other miners in Park County objected to the hiring of the Chinese on the grounds that, as they said, the Chinese could be hired for less money than whites. Such was not the case. Rather, the Chinese were better workers and thus could compete more strongly for jobs. When the Mosquito Pass road was being built, a furor arose over rumors that Chinese were doing the construction, but the charges were denied.

The 1880 census showed that in Park County, with a total population of about 4,000, there were 124 Chinese—almost two-thirds being laborers, almost one-third being miners, and the rest being laundry workers. cooks, and housekeepers. One man was a water carrier, and two were labor contractors—Lin Sou and Ah Ping. There was one little girl.

The Chinese carrier provided Fairplay with its first water system. Water was hauled, even to the hospital, in five-gallon coal oil cans hung on shoulder yokes. The going rate was two dollars to fill a 54-gallon whiskey barrel. "China Mary" ran a laundry on Front Street and was a well-loved member of the village. Another Chinese laundry was on Main Street. "Little Mary" sold vegetables.

Most of the Chinese lived across the gulch from Fairplay in about twenty one-room houses built in a row with a common wall between each. Every house had a door and one window in front under a little peaked roof. Each morning the men met at the *tong* house to get their day's work assignments. Lin Sou, who spoke English, managed the men with ability. He had also been in charge at Blackhawk.

159

After Thayer took a good share of the Chinese to Como, some still remained in Fairplay. Some worked the Cincinnati Placer above Fairplay, paying a dollar a day to the placer owner and, in turn, keeping all the gold they recovered. In 1881 about twenty were working placers back toward Frederick Mountain. When a group of white men approached one day, a gunfight occurred in which one Chinese was killed. Apparently the Chinese were beginning to recognize claim jumpers when they saw them and, armed with guns, had hurried to defend themselves.

The lower end of Beaver Creek, the whole length of which had been taken up in placer claims, was eventually bought up by the Platte River Placer Company and worked hydraulically. Then in the 1920's dredging was introduced on Beaver Creek. A dredge boat, which was built on the creek, was still working, but only about half time, in 1940.

In the 1920's the South Park Dredging Company began its operations of the Platte southeast of Fairplay. Built in California and patterned on the huge dredges used there, the new boat used on the Platte was 510 feet long by sixty-eight feet wide, including stacker and ladder. The ladder supported 132 dredge buckets which fed gravel from the bottom of the river into the dredge, where the ore was milled. The stacker dumped the masticated tailings along the channel. As the buckets scooped up about thirty-five bites per minute, the whole dredge would move slowly along at about six feet in four hours.

At its peak the dredge sent enough amalgam each week to Fairplay to retort one $6,500-ingot. The product was eighty-four per cent gold and sixteen per cent silver. Dredging continued until World War II and then resumed from 1945 until 1952, when it could no longer operate at a profit. The operation did not drastically affect the economy of the area since only a twenty-five-man force was required to run the dredge. The despoiled ground may even cost Fairplay more than the town received in payroll when it counts the unreclaimed land and the loss of scenic beauty.

With the dredge, Fairplay's own mining activity ended. The grave of Prunes the Burro on the main street memorializes not only the little beast who shared many decades of the region's mining but also an era that had passed. Not much of that former town remains. Even the Fairplay Hotel is a relative newcomer, having been built in 1923 after the old one burned. The hotel's magnificent mahogany bar is an import from Rachel's Place in Alma. Rachel's Place itself and many other historic buildings of South Park preserve the old-time atmosphere in the South Park City restoration.

The Fairplay Hotel and later the Hand Hotel both were operated in the more recent years by the Hands. Grandma Hand, as Mrs. Hand was affectionately called, became well known for her hospitality. She also was known for her impressive collection of Indian artifacts which she found in South Park and her equally impressive ability to catch large trout in the area's streams.

Colonel Frank Mayer, who lived the last ten of his 103 years in Fairplay, was another of Fairplay's better known citizens. Mayer's life had seen him as a Civil War drummer boy, a soldier in the Middle East, a buffalo hunter (about which he co-authored a book), a rancher in Montezuma County, and finally a resident of Park County. He lived at the Snowstorm Placer near Alma for sixteen years before coming to Fairplay. Many of the arrowheads in Grandma Hand's collection were acquired from Colonel Mayer.

THE TARRYALL DISTRICT

The story of the old Tarryall district has not been finished. Hamilton did not completely expire in the 1860's. In 1870 there were about thirty pupils in its school. Dunbar's and Link's hotels still provided lodging or meals for stage passengers in 1871, and Wells Fargo maintained an express depot at Hamilton for the region as late as 1872. In the early 1870's there were ten families and one "marriageable young lady." As mining activity increased during the decade, the population grew to about 100 in 1877; there were still two hotels and Blandin's general merchandise store. Not until the railroad came through Como in 1879 did most of Hamilton's former population move out to the new town two miles away. However, Hamilton still had a post office in 1880 but in part for people farther up the gulch.

The *Daily Central City Register* reported that eight companies with thirty employees were working the valley in 1871. (In addition, George W. Lechner had two men working in Park Gulch below Como and was attempting to open up a coal vein besides.) The Tarryall mines extended upstream into Little French Gulch. The Tarryall companies belonged to Leland Peabody; Curtice and Hibbard; Barrett, Hall, and Rische; and the Liebelt Brothers, among others.

By 1878 Hall, Barrett, and Rische had brought two or three dozen Chinese workers into the Tarryall placers. Working the area even into the 1900's, the Chinese occupied cabins at Hamilton as they were abandoned. Augmented by the Chinese who were employed in Como's coal fields, Hamilton became a China Town with about 200 orientals living there. A dredge operation which reworked the placers around the turn of the century took out the cabins that remained in Hamilton as well as the big stage line barn.

A short distance upstream, where the road forks off to Boreas Pass, was the site of Leland Peabody's placer, worked through the 1870's and 1880's. For the summer of 1879 Peabody employed fifteen men, netting $7,000. The next year and for the next ten years Peabody hired Chinese, employing Alfred S. Turner (whose family figures in the story of South Park ranching) to supervise them. Today tidy rock terraces around a few of the remaining shacks at Peabody's recall the Chinese who must have laid out the landscaping.

At the fork of North and South Tarryall Creeks, just above Peabody's, was the original Tarryall discovery and the later Fortune Placer. About 1890 John Fortune began operating the placer there by hand. In 1912 he converted to hydraulic mining despite the scarcity of water which had always curtailed mining in the gulch. Although the Fortune Placer produced half of all the gold ever found in the gulch, by 1917 costs of labor and equipment forced him to quit; but, in addition, his decision was precipitated by an injunction brought against the placer by ranchers in the

162

park. As the placer had extended its size with miles of ditches and pipes, the loss of water from the creek and the dumping of debris and tailings into it elicited the complaints of ranchers and the Isaak Walton League. However, the Fortune was worked again briefly in the 1930's by the Jewell Placers Company.

Montgomery Gulch—not at Montgomery but along a tributary of the Tarryall north of Mt. Silverheels—developed after 1880. In 1896 gold strikes brought an influx of 150 men. Four tunnels were soon dug. A smelter was erected in Montgomery Gulch in 1925, but it did not operate long. Today there is active mining at this location on Mt. Silverheels.

Farther on, deep against the "Snowy Range," the Liebelt Placer was worked in Little French Gulch until 1925. The Liebelt was second only to the Fortune Placer. Denver newspapers dated as late as 1938 line old cabin walls at Little French Gulch, indicating some activity in the valley at that recent time.

Today beaver ponds, lodgepole pines and Engelmann spruce, Canada jays, and darting grey ouzels have pre-empted Tarryall Gulch. Snow sifts down on fallen aspen leaves, once golden. Silence has laid claim on the old placers.

COMO

Nearby Como, in the meantime, was the scene of a mining industry of a much different nature. As noted previously, George W. Lechner, who was one of the locators of the Snow Blind District, had bought the old Stubbs Ranch, which dated back at least to early 1861, and was attempting to open up coal deposits there. A letter to the Honorable Henry M. Teller from Lechner in 1876 indicated that the latter was delivering coal from his mine to Fairplay and elsewhere daily. However, because of a swindle by a land company Lechner was hard pressed for funds and unable to pay off a loan from Teller. Lechner originally had paid $6,000 for 2,000 acres of patented land along the coal veins and had since put $3,000 into improvements. He further noted in his plea to Teller for more funds that this land was on the proposed line of the Denver, South Park and Pacific. In due course of time he received additional money from Teller.

Lechner's first mine was a mile and a half northwest of Como. A second and bigger mine was located three miles southeast of Como at King, as the place was later called. (W. H. King was a county clerk and the manager and postmaster at a company store in King.)

When Como became temporary end of track for railroad construction that summer, the population of the roaring tent city leaped to 6,000. European coal miners, mostly Italians, were among them. The Italians christened the pond south of town Lake Como and Lechner laid out the town of Como.

In 1879 the South Park Coal Company bought the mines with the Denver, South Park, and Pacific owning 87.5 per cent of the stock. The South Park Coal Company owned 3,000 acres of land and was taking out a good grade of coal, about three-fifths coke and two-fifths volatile matter. In 1879 the coal company began to employ Chinese laborers from Hamilton as well as others brought in from outside the park. The other miners were not pleased with this policy; and, when the company attempted to replace two Italians who had been fired with Chinese, the Italian ranks armed themselves and threatened all of the orientals to leave Como. Thayer, the labor manager, was soundly beaten up for his intervention in behalf of the Chinese, who were advised to leave for a cooling-off period. The sheriff with an armed force then rounded up thirty of the Italian ringleaders and shipped them out of the park on the new railroad.

The Chinese were hired back, their pay being that of the Italians—$2.50 a day. The issue of the use of Chinese labor had been taken up by Coloradans in general, particularly the Denver newspapers. Therefore, the fact that the Chinese miners were not hired as "cheap labor" but as superior workers was made much of by John Evans, president of the DSP&P and of the coal company. His chief opponent in the public debate was William A. H. Loveland, owner of the *Rocky Mountain News*, and, as an executive of the Colorado Central Railway, Evans' adversary in railroad building. Later, when the Union Pacific gained control of the DSP&P and the South Park Coal Company with it, the new owners continued to use about 125 Chinese miners.

By 1880, the railroad construction having been pushed west and completed, Como had settled into a town of 134. Most of the Chinese were living at Hamilton while two hundred or more white miners were living at King, or the "Lower Mine" as it was still called. Even there the population was divided according to nationalities with the Americans and English reigning in the south end of town while the southern Europeans occupied the other end of the place. The mining company had built about sixty frame houses to accommodate them. The town also had a saloon, several stables and a blacksmith shop, a carpenter shop, and powder and scale houses for the mine. Two miles east of town the Thomas Hotel, the new name of the former Eight-Mile House, offered a run-down sort of gathering place and station for teamsters into the area.

In 1881 the Como Iron, Coal and Land Company was organized with Lechner as one of the subscribers. Directors included David H. Moffat, Jr., and the ubiquitous H. A. W. Tabor.

Several additional mines were opened by the Union Pacific at King, the UP having gained control of the Denver and South Park. King continued to be the center of production despite the new operation at Como. The King mines were slope mines in which the coal was brought up to a central slope by mules. A cable powered by a steam engine moved the coal up the main slope.

Explosive gas made the mines at Como among the most treacherous of coal operations in Colorado. In 1885 thirty-five Chinese miners were killed by an explosion in the Como (or King) No. 1 mine. No attempt was made to remove the bodies. The other seven levels of the mine were worked until 1890 when it was closed. This mine had a fire in 1886 and another in 1889, contributing to the abandonment of the mine. In 1893 an explosion in Como (or King) No. 5, the principal mine, killed twenty-five Italians. Many of their bodies were taken to the Como cemetery.

Around 1896 the King mines shut down completely, the post

office closing in that year. Some of the company houses were moved to Como and others were torn down for lumber or firewood. Nothing remains of the town today.

Como continued to exist as a railroad center, being the largest town in South Park from 1890 until 1910 (see Chapter VIII). Its population during that period was about 400. A few Chinese who remained in Como ran laundries, which served double purpose for gambling. They also are remembered for putting on memorable New Year's displays of fireworks. They roasted pigs in a communal, round, mud oven, which captured the attention of local occidentals, too.

Como had three newspapers in its history: the Como *Headlight* from 1883 to 1888, the Park County *Democrat* briefly in 1887 and 1888, and the Como *Record* from 1889 to 1905. There were three hotels at one time and eight saloons.

There were four or five churches and from 1879 to 1948 a school. In fact, there were two schools. Uniquely, the larger school building at Como was the grade school, whereas the one-room schoolhouse near it was the high school.

In the mining story of South Park, Como's coal industry was an isolated instance. With its end in the mid-1890's and the shutdown of most of the silver mines after 1893, South Park mining dropped off sharply. After the repeal of the Sherman Silver Purchase Act in 1893 and the silver deflation which followed, silver mining was in the doldrums everywhere in Colorado and the West. New gold discoveries at Cripple Creek, therefore, drew many of the miners from the old areas to Pikes Peak and its nearby foothills.

BALFOUR

The one mining district which opened up within South Park as a result of the renewed interest in gold mining was Balfour. Balfour also was the only mining town established in the south end of the park, with the exception of Whitehorn which was in Fremont County.

Balfour was located about ten miles south of Hartsel and about thirty miles west of the Cripple Creek district. It was southwest of the Currant Creek Pass road to Guffey and Canon City and on the north bank of Buffalo Slough.

The site was first prospected in 1866 when good assays were made but, for some unknown reason, not developed. In November of 1893 the town of Balfour was founded. An immediate subject of hot but one-sided debate about hiring mine workers reflected feeling concerning the labor problems at the north end of the park. A meeting was held in Balfour in January of 1894 at which diatribes were delivered by men who had worked at Aspen, Leadville, and other camps. At the close of the testimonials, the assembly passed a resolution to forbid Chinese and Italians from entering the camp.

In November a weekly newspaper, the Balfour *News*, first appeared, published by James Lightfoot and Joe Swan. It was printed until 1897. In the spring of 1894 the population of the town, perhaps stimulated more by unemployment elsewhere than by rich ore at Balfour, had grown to 800. Two stages daily stopped there. There were three hotels—the Balfour, the Clarendon, and the Crawford Hotel and Restaurant. Stores and the Nugget Saloon were in full swing, and 110 log or frame buildings had gone up. Later, at its peak, Balfour had about 200 houses. To supply lumber Tom Gill ran a sawmill. He also had one of the stores, his two enterprises both being moved to Bath on Trout Creek Pass after Balfour's brief flurry.

Most of the debris marking the empty townsite is found quite close to Colorado Route 9, although a handful of buildings are scattered back along the slough to a point where a dam was built. A ditch carried water from the small reservoir to the location of what evidently was a small mill. Otherwise, there are few clues to the town of Balfour.

The similiarity of the volcanic geology of the Balfour area and Cripple Creek produced more and more interest but less and less gold, apparently. In December, 1896, Balfour had become a fourth class post office, an office which still was noted in 1906 on a postal map; and in the winter of 1898-99 Alice Wonder had taught school there before her stint at Leavick. One might suppose that Balfour began to dwindle away around 1900.

With Balfour and the nineteenth century the era of the independent pick-and-shovel miner had ended. As had been the case with the trappers, a few isolated miners lingered back in the hills —more because that was their way of life than because they still hoped for glittering riches. Twentieth-century mining, the scattered operations that amounted to anything, were a corporate, industrial kind of business, more akin to factories than to the gold rush of 1859.

Another age had come and gone in South Park.

CHAPTER EIGHT

A Half Century of Railroading

Just as South Park's location had resulted in its being criss-crossed by trails and wagon roads, so too it presented a logical route for railroads. First the narrow-gauge tracks of the Denver, South Park and Pacific entered the park from Denver by way of the Platte Canyon, and later the broad-gauged Colorado Midland reached the area from Colorado Springs by way of Ute Pass.

The DSP&P route was originally considered as early as 1868, when railroads were first being projected through the West. At that time Governor Evans envisioned Denver as a great rail center. He proposed a network of lines, including one to run up Platte Canyon to South Park and on to the Blue River. In addition, in 1868 a survey was run from Denver to Santa Fe by way of the Platte River, South Park, and Trout Creek Pass.

In 1872 the budding Denver, South Park and Pacific set out ambitiously for South Park. The route from Denver for the narrow gauge was planned to be by way of Bear Creek to Buffalo Creek and so to South Park because the lower Platte Canyon was thought to be too difficult. However, the railroad's advance was only as far as the site of Morrison where the railroad investors also owned quarries which were to be exploited. The original officers and directors in these enterprises are familiar names in Colorado history—Evans, Cheesman, Kountz, and Moffat as well as others.

Immediately it was evident that the line was not going to go

169

any farther without more funds, so the citizens of Arapahoe County voted a bond issue of $300,000 to assist it; but the Panic of 1873 brought all activity to a halt while the voters protested the failure to build. Frank Hall defended the DSP&P's officers in his *History of Colorado* by pointing out that the company was faced with construction along a route that offered no settlement from Littleton all the way to Fairplay, no cultivation, and a mining region in which production had been sharply reduced in the past decade. There were only the stone quarries in the Front Range and the prospect of timbering for immediate revenue.

As a result, the best service which the DSP&P could offer for a few years was a train ride to Morrison with a transfer to a stage from that point for the major part of the trip. Nevertheless, the first engines optimistically bore the names of "Fairplay" and "Platte Canon."

In 1876 construction did begin in Platte Canyon. As the three-foot line was hacked and hued out of the canyon walls and the stream bed, fishermen, excursionists, and summer people climbed aboard and moved into the mountains with it. By 1878 the DSP&P had reached Pine Grove, then Estabrook, then Buffalo Creek. Pine Grove for years was to be a lunch stop on the line.

In January of 1879 Webster on the east side of Kenosha Pass became the railhead and soon developed into a rip-snorting camp fit for a TV horse opera. At Webster stages and wagons met the trains to take the traffic over into South Park, while construction crews labored to get the line on up the hill. The tracks doubled back and forth to traverse the two miles of steep grade to the summit.

Work was intense, for the South Park was now in a race. The Denver and Rio Grande was heading up the Arkansas in a marathon to reach Leadville first. When the DSP&P reached the top of Kenosha Pass, it had crews working around the clock. At night torchlight outlined the right of way.

Kenosha was seventy-six miles out of Denver. Here a depot, water tank, and repair shop were built. There were also a wye and more than a half mile of siding, from which many ties were to be shipped. The old Kenosha House was still in existence, remaining until at least 1896. The station stood until 1919.

The west side of the pass called for more than four per cent grade. Consequently, Case Spur was built at the west end of the slope, about two and a half miles from Kenosha Station. The short spur still appeared on a map dated 1913.

In 1879 a new town of Jefferson sprang up as the narrow gauge steamed down across the north end of the park. The railroad built there a wye and a water tank, a frame depot which also served as living quarters for the stationmaster, and a two-story section house. The depot still stands beside the highway at Jefferson. Shortly the new town acquired a post office and express office and the population reached 300 by 1881. Stock pens were added for loading cattle and sheep from the ranches in the northeast corner of the park.

About three and a half miles west of Jefferson was Fox Spur, which still appeared on a 1913 map. Immediately beyond this spur was Michigan Siding. In 1906 it was listed as a station.

Somewhere in the vicinity of Michigan, possibly just west of it, was Dake. Dake was listed in the *Business Directory* of 1884 as having a population of thirty-five and its own post office. An 1898 map shows it on the railroad, about ten miles northeast of Fairplay.

Coal Branch Junction was the next station west of Dake. Three-fourths of a mile east of Como, this was the junction for the branch line which ran to King. The junction also had a wye when the Boreas Pass High Line was built to Leadville so that trains could be turned to back into Como and thus be headed in the right direction for Boreas or Denver. At one time Coal Branch Junction had about two-thirds of a mile of siding.

The branch line to King was a little over three miles long. At King the railroad had a water tank and over a mile of siding for the coal cars. The tracks into King were laid in 1879 and pulled up in 1899. King was originally but briefly called Como by the railroad until the station at the permanent site of Como was built. Then the name King was adopted for the lower mine location (see Chapter VII).

The main line reached Como, eighty-eight miles from Denver, in July of 1879. The tent city of thousands which sprang up blazed even more spectacularly than had Webster as construction camp and end of track for the hordes of adventurers, drifters, and solid citizens scrambling to get to Leadville. Here passengers changed to stages bound for Mosquito or Weston Pass. At Como the railroad quickly built the brick Gilman Hotel in 1880. This two-and-a-half story structure burned in 1896 and was replaced the next year by the large building which still stands beside the abandoned grade. It was a hotel and diningroom at first. The division offices, originally in the large frame depot next to it, were later moved into the ground floor of the big hotel.

The railroad also had a section house, a large water tank, coal bins, an ice house, car shop, lumber shed, blacksmith shop, about two miles of siding, and a six-stall roundhouse built of stone. The roundhouse was moved into Como from an earlier location in Platte Canyon in 1886. By 1880 Como also had a post office and an express office.

Immediately Como gained a reputation not only as a railroad and coal mining center but also as the town which had "furnished the county with a larger proportion of criminal business than any other town," according to the Fairplay Flume in 1882. "Another foul murder" had just been committed at the time of the report. Again, a brakeman who had been fired created a disturbance at Denver's Union Station by hurling rocks at the conductor who was responsible for his dismissal. When the two next met at Como, the conductor, fed up with continuing harassment, shot the former brakeman—only wounding him. And so it continued in Como.

Como grew to about 400 at the turn of the century. About 100 or 150 of its population were employees of the railroad, either as trainmen, headquarters personnel, or shop workers. Next to patronizing the town's numerous pool halls and saloons—especially Delaney's—the most popular sport was baseball. The town had three baseball teams at one time. The men also supported a volunteer fire company with a hose cart, various lodges, and a band.

When most of the shops were destroyed by fire in 1909, they

172

were not rebuilt. In 1911 the roundhouse was closed and Como became nearly deserted. In 1935 the roundhouse too burned, although the stone shell still stood and was used as a warehouse for a dredge company for a time.

As the DSP&P track was laid across South Park in 1879, Red Hill was the next station beyond Como. Red Hill Pass is crossed at about 10,000 feet in altitude, west of Como on U.S. 285. The station was on the west shoulder of the ridge and about a mile or two south of the present highway. The total distance from Como to Red Hill station was six miles.

In August, 1880, a fire broke out in the new Red Hill depot, exploding 1,000 pounds of powder. The assistant station agent was killed, and four others were injured. The entire settlement— five buildings—was destroyed. The depot was rebuilt, and Red Hill became an important station on the line; for here passengers and freight were transferred to Fairplay, Leadville, and Breckenridge until rails reached those towns. Traffic to Alma, Dudley, Mosquito, and the many other camps in the northwest portion of the park added to the bustle at Red Hill.

Red Hill never had a post office, its population boasting no more than about twenty-five. The station operated into the 1900's, but nothing remains of the site today.

From Red Hill the line swung south down Trout Creek (not to be confused with the better known stream running down to the Arkansas). The creek flows between two ridges, the eastern one separating Trout Creek from the Tarryall drainage and the western one separating the creek from the Middle Fork of the South Platte. Trout Creek and the narrow gauge emerged from the grassy valley at Garo.

Between Red Hill and Garo were Hay Ranch, Burrow's Spur, and Arthurs. Hay Ranch, four miles south of Red Hill, had a frame section house and a siding. It operated as late as 1906, when it was still listed. Burrow's Spur was merely a very short spur two and a half miles beyond Hay Ranch and probably served a local ranch. It was in use around 1912.

Two and a half miles farther down the track was Arthurs, a 320-foot siding from which considerable hay was shipped. In

1884 Arthurs had a population of twenty-five. The ranch served by the siding belonged to E. P. Arthur, an Englishman who had taken up the property in 1874. This was the same E. P. Arthur who, with C. G. Hathaway, opened the Bank of Alma.

Below Arthurs the tracks crossed the Adolf Guiraud ranch and passed through the water gap cut by the South Platte to bring the line onto the western segment of South Park. On the south bank of the Platte the railroad built the station called Garos—a misspelled tribute to the local rancher, one of South Park's first homesteaders. (The railroads so frequently changed the spelling of family names and place names for their stations that one supposes that the alterations were deliberate so as to avoid legal difficulties.)

In subsequent years, when the Alma Branch was built from Garos, the station's importance grew. It was to have a depot, a two-story section house, coal bins for the engines, stock pens, a large water tank and a windmill to fill the tank, and more than a half-mile of siding. The depot was behind the store building which is one of the few remaining structures of the old town of Garo. A post office and express offices were established at Garo in 1880 and housed in the store when it was moved there in 1885.

The point at once became a terminal for stages from Colorado Springs and Canon City. Coaches left these towns early in the morning and arrive at Garos late in the afternoon of the next day, in time to catch the daily trains west. Being located in superb game and fish country, Garos also attracted sportsmen from Denver who could arrive by train in a day. Trainmen accommodated the passengers by stopping the train to load any game that happened to be shot from the train windows as the narrow gauge chugged along through the park.

Around the station about a dozen houses sprang up to create the town of Garo. A school was built to serve neighboring children—whether they wanted to be served or not. And Stevens' saloon was built to serve a more willing segment of the population. In 1885 Chubb Newitt moved his store in on two flat cars from his old town at Chubb's Ranch, later called Newitt, on the west side of Trout Creek Pass. Chubb was postmaster and store-keeper for thirteen years.

The front door of this store formerly was on what is now the rear of the building, and thus it was accessible to the depot and train tracks, the center of activity. However, not all of the bustle there was routine. For example, one day the station agent, a Mrs. Dittmore, flew off in some sort of a frenzy just as the train puffed into Garos and shot herself. Another station agent, a male, was responsible for the demise of Chubb Newitt. The agent strolled into the store one day to pass the time with the other neighborhood gossips. As he idly tried the heft of one of the guns on sale, he accidentally shot Newitt in the posterior. Newitt died later of blood poisoning.

Garos survived longer than other stations down the track; for, after rails were abandoned to the south and over Trout Creek Pass in 1926, the Alma Branch still remained in operation until 1937.

About three and a half miles southwest of Garos was the short-lived but spectacular camp of Weston—end of track for the Denver and South Park for a few months beginning in October, 1879. This point had been reached in only five months as the railroad hurried across South Park from Kenosha Pass. In the South Park's marathon to reach Leadville, it spawned three notorious end-of-track towns—Webster, Como, and Weston—in that order in terms of geography, chronology, and sheer debauchery. Local rumor has it that Weston was burned by Indians. However, Weston did not need that fictitious ending to its flaming history. It is easy to suppose that, after burning its candles at both ends for six months, the place died a natural death. At any rate, there were no Indians in South Park in 1880.

Thousands of construction workers and drifters roamed the town. There were fifteen eating houses and saloons, including the Oyster Bar and Johnny Nugent's Tontine, where a fellow could come in and get warm from the ravages of winter and loneliness at any time of the day or night. Nugent, who also owned a stage stop in Mosquito Gulch on the Denver-Leadville stage road, moved his popular place from Weston to Newett on Trout

Creek Pass as the DSP&P progressed westward. (Nugent later had celebrated places also in Manitou Springs and Cripple Creek.)

The wickedest of all, though, was Frank Morgan, who owned a combination saloon, gambling house, and dance hall. In Morgan's employ were twenty females of assorted talents. Morgan also gained the reputation of being the town's leading sharpshooter. He bragged that he had drawn his gun twenty times to shoot and as many times had celebrated the death of an enemy.

Piled high amid this diabolical confusion were unsheltered mounds of machinery and supplies on their way to Leadville, and bullion on its way from the silver camp to Denver. Weston was not only the end of track for the railroad, but it was also a junction for wagon roads. The enormous freight traffic from Wilkerson Pass ran through Hartsel to Weston and thence to Platte Station. From Platte Station roads led over Weston Pass or north to Fairplay and Hoosier Pass. Another road from Weston went southwest to Trout Creek Pass. Three transfer companies handled the major part of the huge freight business that centered in Weston during the winter of 1880. Spotswood was the foremost of the three and was transporting 100 passengers daily to Leadville besides. Despite all of this activity, Weston was not a post office and received its mail from Platte Station.

When the railroad pushed on over Trout Creek Pass, Weston—and the Weston Pass freighting route as well—was abandoned. In later years a railroad tie contractor, Sam Cohen, had a four-car spur near the location of Weston. Other than a few old foundations, rubbish piles, and the town's small cemetery, Weston is completely gone today.

About three miles beyond Weston railroad maps indicated a gravel pit, dating around the 1890's. Another mile down the track, eight miles southwest of Garo, was Platte River Tank and, about a mile farther, Platte River. (Platte River station on the DSP&P is not the same Platte Station on the Weston Pass wagon road.) Platte River had a depot, telegraph office, section house, bunkhouse, a large water tank, coal bins, stock pens, and a half mile of siding. This station, located just north of Antero Reservoir, was the last stop for the South Park before the trains began the

A narrow-gauge engine pauses for the camera man on the west side of Kenosha Hill. *Courtesy of the Library, State Historical Society of Colorado, Charles Weitfle photo.*

A load of ties heads down into South Park from Kenosha Hill. *Courtesy of the Library, State Historical Society of Colorado.*

The new camp of Jefferson was end of track in 1879 when this photograph was taken with a miniature Denver and South Park passenger train in the background. *Courtesy of the Denver Public Library Western Collection.*

The station at Jefferson stands sentinel beside the Denver and South Park tracks in 1937, the year of their abandonment. *Courtesy of the Denver Public Library Western Collection, M. C. Poor photo.*

A panorama of Como about 1900 shows the roundhouse and coal dock and a train steaming off across the park toward Denver. At the far left the two-storied railroad hotel and dining room can be made out with the station to its right and the building which housed the division offices directly below the hotel. Later the hotel was used for the division headquarters. *Courtesy of the Library, State Historical Society of Colorado.*

181

A somewhat earlier picture of Como gives more detail of the railroad yards and the little town which "furnished the county with a larger proportion of criminal business than any other town" in the early 1880's. The hose company tower is at the extreme left. *Courtesy of the Denver Public Library Western Collection.*

The hotel and headquarters building still stands solidly with the Como station beside it in 1965.

Although weathered lettering on the siding of this abandoned building indicates that it was a store in later years, the "brand" above the door advertises the Diamond Bar, just one of many in a town where both railroad men and coal miners waged a constant battle with thirst.

One of Como's several dance halls underwent a conversion to become the Episcopal Church before the town was deserted. *George White photo.*

This view of the High Line is about two miles above Como along Tarryall Creek near the Peabody Switch. The Peabody Placer workings are seen along the creek. The track crosses the creek and circles back to wind around Windy Point on the upper right. *George White collection, Dr. C. H. Scott photo.*

A camera stop on the High Line at Windy Point. *George White collection.*

185

A view toward Boreas Pass on the High Line grade.

These great, weathered timbers are the skeletons of snow fences which were built between Selkirk and Boreas along the High Line. The twisting road follows the abandoned grade. Red Mountain in the background is to the left of Boreas Pass.

A summer storm builds up behind Boreas Mountain and the abandoned buildings at Boreas station.

A mixed train stands at the Fairplay station on the Alma Branch of the Denver, South Park and Pacific. *Courtesy of the Denver Public Library Western Collection, William H. Jackson photo.*

London Junction in 1889. This station name was shortly changed to Alma Junction. *Courtesy of the Denver Public Library Western Collection.*

The Colorado Midland depot at Hartsel. *Frank Turner collection.*

It was a glorious day for tourists, though a h a r d one for flowers, when the Midland's Wildflower Excursion trains ran to S o u t h Park. *Courtesy of the Pikes Peak Regional District Library.*

191

With water low in Elevenmile Canyon Reservoir, the old grade of the Colorado Midland and the bed of the South Platte River once again appear.

pull up Trout Creek Pass. Therefore, it was an important facility although it was not a town as such.

Platte River's mail was delivered at Buffalo Springs, a nearby ranch and resort spot. Buffalo Springs had a hotel as well as the post office in 1881. However, its population was only twenty in 1884, and the place apparently expired soon thereafter.

The DSP&P tracks climbed seven miles on an easy grade out of Platte River station to Hilltop station at the crest of the pass, 120 miles from Denver and 9,516 feet above sea level. The population of about twenty-five which lived there were all employed on the railroad. There were a depot, telegraph office, bunkhouses, a section house, and about half a mile of siding. Mail came from Platte Station. Some lumbering and ranching were carried on around Trout Creek Pass, and operators loaded their ties and cattle there.

From the top of the pass the line ran down Trout Creek to the Arkansas River, reaching the valley in February of 1880. However, by 1879 Jay Gould had gained a half interest in the rival Denver and Rio Grande and also gained control of the DSP&P in 1880, bringing the latter into his Union Pacific system. As a result of the organizational shenanigans that ensued, the valiant race across South Park was in vain; for it was determined that the D&RG would be the line to build up the Arkansas into Leadville, the Denver and South Park being allowed to use those tracks under a "Joint Operating Agreement." The DSP&P then started off across the mountains toward Gunnison in another losing race with the D&RG.

Evidently the UP considered the Joint Operating Agreement an interim arrangement, for it very soon projected a line from Como over Boreas Pass to Leadville by way of Breckenridge. The plan was to tap the Summit County traffic and to hook up with the Colorado Central which ran from Denver through Georgetown. This link was never to be made, however. But the Boreas Pass "High Line" not only was completed to Leadville but survived the original main line for a decade. The Boreas route, branching off at Como, added greatly to the activity of that town.

Construction of the Boreas line commenced out of Como in

April, 1881, while the D&RG predictably raced north out of Leadville over Fremont Pass to get to the Blue River first. The High Line's route to the top of Boreas Pass was ten miles in length with grades up to four per cent. From Boreas to Breckenridge the line descended 1,925 feet in eleven twisting miles. The D&RG was in Dillon on the Blue River a month ahead of the other line and promptly cancelled the Joint Operating Agreement while the Denver and South Park struggled up Fremont Pass to reach the silver city. For the time being, the South Park was out in the cold; but, when its road was finished, it had a route to Leadville from Denver about half as long as the D&RG's Royal Gorge route. Having to cross the Continental Divide twice, however, meant that the South Park still had not gained the advantage. The route also lacked lucrative cities along the way, such as the D&RG had.

To trace the route from Como to Boreas, the necessary limits of a history of South Park, one starts at Coal Spur. A one-mile spur from Como northwest to the Lechner mine had been built in 1880. After the High Line's track was laid in 1882, the junction for this spur was called Coal Spur. It was still operating in the mid-1890's.

At the Peabody Placer the narrow-gauge tracks made a wide, hairpin curve to start the climb out of the Tarryall Creek valley. At Peabody's, or Tarryall as the station was first called, the line had a wye and a nineteen-car spur which served the placers there and farther up the valley.

A number of trains came down toward Peabody's in an unscheduled manner. A freight overturned at Windy Point above the station in the 1890's, as did another a little farther up the line. A trainload of logs piled up between Peabody's and Como during the same period. In 1905 one of the line's best-known and best-loved engineers, Buddy Schwartz, was killed when his engine overturned at Halfway, above Peabody's. A baggage car flipped off the track and took a passenger train with it in 1926, and two years later another engineer was killed when his light freight ran away coming down the steep grade.

The new gravel road which, for the most part, follows the

old railroad grade has circumvented the treacherous Windy Point section by cutting around Davis Overlook. The auto road rejoins the abandoned right of way and passes the location of Halfway, a station at 10,548 feet. At Halfway there were a large water tank, a siding, a section house, and a bunkhouse.

Two and a half miles above Halfway and an equal distance below Boreas were the Selkirk Spur and water tank. This lonely tank, some distance from any headquarters for line crews, was filled with water from Selkirk Creek by means of a steam pump which had to be fired up with coal. Every two or three days some-one had to hike to the tank to take care of this chore—summer or winter. A point on the line called Flanders around 1930 evidently was just a new name for Selkirk.

Although ten snowsheds once sheltered the track between Selkirk and Boreas, all traces of these are now gone. One still can see timbers of huge snow fences on the denuded mountain slope, though. Often a tree trunk was simply left standing to serve as an upright for the fences.

The tracks crossed Boreas Pass at 11,493 feet above sea level and about ninety-nine miles out of Denver. There were a telegraph office, stone engine house with a turntable, coal bins, and a water tank at one time.

Snowsheds covered the main line and a side track, and a similar covered passageway led into the station for the benefit of passengers and trainmen at this frigid, wind-swept station; for the name of the pass had been changed to Boreas, honoring the god of the north wind, with good reason. When the line closed down for the winter of 1910-1911, mountain lions moved into these tunnels and had to be evicted when operations resumed in the spring. The sheds burned in 1934. The entire station had narrowly escaped being burned in June, 1893, when an enormous forest fire raged on the mountains above for two days. Although most of the buildings now are gone, the two-story bunkhouse remains.

When one looks at the skeletons of the giant snow fences to the north of the station and tries to visualize the weather that necessitated them, the grade and the twisting track that once wound down to Breckenridge, it seems surprising that the High

Line managed to operate at all. But operate it did, being the main line the last years of the South Park's life. The Boreas tracks were abandoned in April, 1937.

At the same time roughly that the High Line construction was started, the UP began to lay out a branch line from Garo to the Mosquito district. In the mid-1870's, while all of South Park's railroads were still merely on paper, the Fairplay, Alma, and Dudley Railroad Company had been formed. This line, as proposed, was to run from Lechner's mine near Como to Fairplay; then to Alma and Dudley; and finally—with high ambitions, to say the least—on to the Moose and Russia mines high on Mt. Bross and Mt. Lincoln.

By 1878 the South Park Railroad Construction and Land Company was investigating Mosquito and Weston Passes in an effort to find a shorter route to Leadville than its Trout Creek survey, and in 1879 the Mosquito Range and Leadville Tunnel and Mining Company also had been incorporated, with Governor Pitkin as figurehead president. Directors included owners of mines on both sides of the Mosquitoes. They also incorporated the Red Hill, Fairplay, and Leadville Railroad Company shortly. The railroad was to connect with the DSP&P at Red Hill and, of course, to use the proposed tunnel to connect to Leadville. However, an estimated $4,000,000 required for tunnel construction ended that proposal.

When the Alma Branch was built in 1881, it was done by the UP and was a much more down-to-earth affair. Its terminal was neither the top of Mt. Lincoln nor Leadville but the London Mine. It is possible that the UP also had a weather-eye out, though, for an entry into the Leadville traffic, so near to and yet so far from Mosquito Gulch. Indeed, in 1882, after the tracks had reached the London Mine, rumors again flew to the effect that the mine owners were going to go through the range with the railroad. In 1883 the Fairplay, Mt. Sheridan, and Leadville Railroad was incorporated, persisting in the same idea, though with the route moved south to Four Mile Creek and Iowa Gulch. But after the first flush of enthusiasm for railroad building, economic facts killed forever the idea of a Mosquito Range tunnel.

196

Fairplay failed to cooperate with the railroad builders, just as Park County had once refused to help finance road improvements on the Mosquito Pass route. Perhaps Fairplay was still chafing because the DSP&P main line had bypassed the county seat. At any rate, when the Alma Branch was laid out, it was denied a right of way through Fairplay; therefore, the tracks swung around the north side of town.

The line from Garo to Fairplay ran northwest along the Middle Fork of the South Platte. Between Garo and Fairplay the railroad maintained two facilities. One of these, six miles southeast of Fairplay, was a four-car spur called Platte Ranch. It evidently was used by the local ranch of that name. Called Platte Ranch around 1912, it was Myers at an earlier time. Immediately beyond Platte Ranch was the Lime Rock Tank. Perhaps what Rand McNally called Lime Rock Track in 1896 was just another name for a spur at that location.

At Fairplay the road built a brick and frame depot with generous loading platforms for the busy town which had snubbed it. The depot served passengers and freight. In addition, the line had two section houses and two thousand feet of siding at Fairplay.

Three miles above Fairplay was Roberts, possibly a ranch facility. It was listed in a postal guide for 1896 but may have been a single outfit as its mail was delivered at Fairplay. Snowstorm, where the Platte River Placer Company owned a short spur, was about a mile above Roberts.

Another mile above Snowstorm was London Junction. The Alma Branch did not go into Alma but stopped short of it below town at London Junction, where the line turned off into the Mosquito District. The station at the junction was called Alma Junction after 1895. All of the supplies for Alma had to be hauled by wagon the intervening half mile, and the additional trouble and expense must have itched longer and worse than any Mosquito bite in history. The Alma smelter, however, built a short spur from the junction.

The section between Fairplay and London Junction was overseen by foreman "Old Bill" McFee. McFee, of broad-gauged dimensions himself, would settle his bulk on a little four-wheeled, narrow-gauged flatcar and ride the line delivering materials. His motive power was provided by a burro called Vanderbilt, technically designated as a "long-eared 0-4-0." The Vanderbilt-McFee consist was a familiar sight around the turn of the century.

At London Junction the frame depot also served as living quarters for the station agent. The station was on the west side of the present highway. The branch maintained coal bins, a large water tank, a scale house, and a half mile of siding here. By 1883 a town of 200 people had grown up at the junction while two sampling works also had located there.

In 1882 the branch called the London Mine Railroad was completed up Mosquito Gulch all the way to the mill at the foot of the North London Mine. A station at Park City, three miles above London Junction, served the Orphan Boy, Hock-Hocking, and other neighboring mines, as well as the colorful population of the place. Park City apparently never had a depot as such, though. In 1908 the C&S built a spur at the junction of North and South Mosquito Creeks into the big smelter at the South London Mine.

The Alma Junction depot was closed in 1924. Primarily because of the London Mine ore freight, combined with Alma's and Fairplay's traffic, the Alma Branch survived until 1937, although revenue was not enough to keep the railroad operating in the black.

The Leavick Branch came off the Alma Branch at a point a mile below Fairplay. About twelve miles long, the line was built in 1895 and shared in the mining activity of the Horseshoe district. The branch officially was called the Denver, South Park, and Hilltop Railroad—"Hilltop" referring to the rich Hilltop Mine on Mt. Sheridan. The junction point below Fairplay was called Hill Top Junction, rather easily confused with the station on Trout Creek Pass, which a few years earlier had been Hilltop, but now was called Summit.

For many years the Leavick Branch had a spur at Pearts' ranch, four miles from Hill Top Junction. Pearts' ranch was one of the older and better known outfits in the area. The owner,

198

John Pearts, worked the small Crusader Mine on Horseshoe Mountain in addition to his ranch operation.

Four miles above Pearts' was Horseshoe station (see Chapter VII). Poor says that Horseshoe station was also called East Leadville at times. Actually, the place was neither Horseshoe nor East Leadville but Mudsill. The short spur at Mudsill (or Horseshoe or East Leadville) served the Mudsill Mine to the northwest. This mine and East Leadville both were off the main gulch of Fourmile Creek as well as the railroad and merely had access at the station. The actual town of Horseshoe was below the Mudsill-Horseshoe-East Leadville station.

Leavick was the terminal for the line. It was three miles above Mudsill station and more than 11,000 feet above sea level. Leavick had a twenty-car siding where ore cars for the big mill were set out.

In 1895 an eastbound train on the branch left the track and the whole outfit overturned. Otherwise, the line seems to have been a fairly routine operation—the sort which attracted little attention but on which the life of the mining district depended.

The diminutive Denver and South Park suffered every kind of difficulty possible. But it was the sentimental favorite of fishermen, hunters, and tourists who liked its custom-fitted stops wherever the best fishing holes, game, or camera views were to be had. Probably its valiant but doomed races with the D&RG at every turn also earned it a certain popularity as the underdog and an indestructible loyalty among its personnel and railroad buffs alike. Furthermore, for many years it served a vital economic role in the life of South Park's towns, mines, and ranches.

Nevertheless, red ink was common on the road's ledgers. The history of its ownership casts the line pretty much in the role of a stepchild. After the UP had gained control, the DSP&P kept its original name until 1890 when it was put within a system known as the Denver, Leadville and Gunnison Railway. Then in 1898 the Colorado and Southern got control of it and gave the road its name. Under the banner of the C&S a portion of the South Park line became part of a fan-shaped network of lines briefly called the Denver and Interurban Railroad Company. (In

199

1906 Gannett designated the London Mine Railroad as the Denver and Interurban.) After ten years with the C&S, the South Park was passed on to the Burlington, though still operating as the C&S. Through these many changes, the line was popularly called the Denver and South Park or, simply, the South Park.

Snow was the biggest problem in operating the line, and the winter of 1899-1900 was the king. On December 17 an engine bucking a storm left the tracks just below Cottage Grove on the way to Alma Junction. That was the last of train operations on that branch until March 17 when the engine was raised and service resumed. For those three months there was no telephone or telegraph service either. Coal oil gave out so there were no lamps. The younger generation at Fairplay amused itself with dances at the Odd Fellows Hall, illuminated with candles strung up around the room with baling wire. Then one of the most popular girls at the dances broke out with measles, followed shortly by all of the rest of the young people in town, and the place settled down to waiting quietly for the branch to re-open.

On January 15 a passenger train which had been stalled at Como finally got through to Leadville where it was again stalled. This was the only passenger train to get through in a two-week period. A rotary and two flangers were trying to keep the line open out of Como, but drifts had reached thirty feet deep in the park. Fifteen engines, tied together, had tried to buck their way through and, as a result, had been off the track there for two weeks. A passenger train derailed on Kenosha Hill for over twenty-four hours, forcing its ticketholders to wade through the drifts to neighboring ranches.

As the weather worsened toward the end of January, service in Platte Canyon was running only as far as Grant. From Grant stages once again carried the few hardy travelers over Kenosha to South Park and to the Blue River region. On February 2 a train finally forced its way from Como over Boreas Pass to Breckenridge, where supplies were running out. And that was the end of service to Breckenridge except by sled until March 9.

As spring arrived the tracks were partially opened here and there, with equipment breaking down, stalling, and blocking the line again as often as not. Then, as the copious supply of snow began to melt, the run-off broke the new dam at Cheesman Lake on the Middle Fork of the South Platte, east of the park, and the ensuing flood took out six miles of track in the lower Platte Canyon. Finally on May 28 the train waiting in Leadville since January got through all the way to Denver.

During the 1920's and 1930's the railroad repeatedly sought abandonment of the line still in operation. Although it was operating in the red, the people of Park County fought its removal successfully—not out of sentiment so much as because the railroad was paying almost one-third of the county's taxes. Tracks finally were pulled up in 1938, a year after operations stopped.

The early struggle of the Denver and South Park to compete with the larger systems was doomed before it began, if the history of Western railroading is any gauge. And as independent lines were taken over by the bigger companies, the mine and mill owners were caught in a monopolistic squeeze with high freight rates and arbitrary traffic policies. Such a predicament undoubtedly accounts for the intense interest among local mine owners in constructing a Mosquito Range tunnel route.

Among the rash of proposed railroads of the period, many were probably the result merely of overly excited investors. South Park—so easy to cross, if one could just ignore the mountains around it—provided a route on paper for many such schemes. As early as 1867 the Colorado Springs and South Park Railroad Company had been proposed to run from the coal mines at that city, up Ute Pass to South Park, and across "Pauncha Pass" to the San Luis Valley. In 1877 the Canon City, Oil Creek, and Fairplay Railroad was organized but with a plan for getting from Canon City to Saguache in the opposite direction, it turned out. Then in 1880 some of the same incorporators put together on paper the Canon City and Western Railroad Company. This time, inspired by the Leadville boom, they remembered to include the route up Oil Creek from the Fremont County coal mines, across South Park to Alma and then, somehow, to Leadville.

At least by 1883 the Rio Grande was eyeing a route across South Park. The plan was to run from Acequia (south of Denver)

201

up the Platte to South Park, entering the park in the southeast corner, the area later occupied by Elevenmile Canyon Reservoir. The route then was to cross the lower end of the park and to drop down into Salida, generally on the route of the old Ute Trail. In 1884 an additional branch was added to the proposal with the idea of bringing tracks up Oil Creek from Canon City to Florissant and so to connect with the line on the South Platte, a few miles west of Florissant. Another D&RG line would run down across Currant Creek Pass and then up the Arkansas to Salida. Nothing came of these many proposals, however.

On the other hand, the Colorado Midland Railway did materialize. It was incorporated in 1883 by men with financial interests in Leadville and Aspen mines. Many of them lived in Colorado Springs. After two years of frustrated efforts to raise adequate funds to build, a new president, James J. Hagerman, was able to attract enough Eastern and British capital to get construction under way.

The route ran from Colorado Springs through Manitou Springs and up the four per cent grades of Ute Pass. After curving around behind Pikes Peak, the line snaked its way down Twin Creek to Florissant and Lake George. At that point the route joined the South Platte River and followed it through Granite Canon, as Elevenmile Canyon originally was called. It then ran across South Park through Hartsel to Trout Creek Pass, down Trout Creek to Buena Vista, and then over the Continental Divide to points west.

Originally the company considered crossing from South Park to the Arkansas River by means of the often-suggested tunnel through the Mosquito Range. That plan being once again rejected, they considered Weston Pass for a right of way but chose Trout Creek instead where grades might run only two per cent instead of three.

The route would have been a good one for the usual mountain railroad, narrow gauges being able to handle relatively steep grades and tight curves. Unfortunately, though, the Colorado Midland was not narrow gauge—it was the first broad-gauged line into the Colorado Rockies. With the exception of the South Park

202

tangents, and even those were a bit swampy in places, the road was expensive to build for broad gauge, difficult to operate, and disappointing financially. With the pre-existing competition of the D&RG and the UP, the railroad was in trouble at the outset.

When grade construction reached Lake George, the D&RG's earlier proposal to build through the canyon loomed as a threat to the Midland. Afraid that the D&RG would perform a repetition of the Royal Gorge battle in Granite Canon, the Midland hastened to get that stretch finished. By the spring of 1887 the grade was complete all the way across South Park to Trout Creek Pass, about eighty-five miles from Colorado Springs. Track was down and the first train to Buena Vista crossed the park in July.

The Colorado Midland's route through South Park served an almost entirely different area than did the DSP&P. Furthermore, since it had only the main line with through trains and no local branches, the CM did not play as intimate a part in the life of South Park as did the other line.

As the Midland first emerged from Granite Canon into the park, many of the trains stopped at Idlewild where, in the low, lush corner of the park, wildflowers were in abundance. The Midland, with an aggressive program to capture passenger traffic, had weekly and, later, daily Wildflower Excursion trains from Colorado Springs. Many of the trains paused at Idlewild to let the passengers collect their bouquets.

At Freshwater, just into the park, there were stock pens for local ranches. This station now is under Elevenmile Canyon Reservoir's waters.

A mile beyond Freshwater station was Howbert, named for a Colorado Springs banker and investor in the Midland. The station included a telegraph office and a large passing track. Howbert was located where ranch buildings now stand at the west outlet of the reservoir. Stages ran from Howbert to Guffey, south of the park. Guffey was then a busy little mining, lumbering, and ranching center. In the early days it was called Freshwater, so one might assume that Freshwater station also was a connecting point for that town. The town of Howbert grew up as a ranch center, and its story rightly is part of Chapter Ten.

Five and a half miles and many crossings of the twisting Platte beyond Howbert was Spinney, named for a well-known rancher of the neighborhood. The Midland had quite extensive facilities at Spinney—a frame station, section house, bunkhouse, a large water tank, coal bins, a passing track, and a wye.

The wye was used for turning the excursion trains, for Spinney was the usual destination of the wildflower train. Here the ladies in fragile dotted Swiss with ruffles and bustles and hoops could yank up the wild iris and penstemon, Indian paintbrush and asters to their hearts' content. Then embellished with a flattering armload of posies, they posed for the photographer before heading back to Colorado Springs.

Almost six miles west of Spinney and seven east of Hartsel, the Midland had a forty-car passing track at a point called Park. As the through trains made up time on the straight tangent east of Hartsel, the track was used by slow freights, no doubt.

Hartsel was a prominent loading point for cattle, sheep, and hay. There were many stock pens there in addition to other facilities. The big frame station, which still stands, housed a waiting room, telegraph office, and freight depot. There also were a large water tank, section house, and bunkhouse.

The Midland gave a hearty boost to business at Hartsel's Hot Springs and the hotel operating there. Also, Hartsel was a popular destination for fishermen and hunters. Morris Cafky repeats an old railroader's report that CM trainmen used to attach a caboose, outfitted for hunting, to the end of a freight headed west out of Colorado Springs. At Hartsel the caboose was set out for the duration of the hunting trip.

Just over a half-mile west of Hartsel the CM had a passing track at a point called Boyer. In 1906 a "special" carrying a party of dignitaries, including Thomas F. Walsh of Camp Bird Mine and Hope Diamond fame, crashed head-on into a freight west of Boyer. The fireman was killed and the engineer and some of the passengers on the special injured.

Antero was a passing track five miles west of Hartsel. Four and a half miles farther on was Haver, directly south of the reservoir. Between Hartsel and Haver was a station called Reinhart, which appears on maps and postal guides only in the 1890's. Haver had a siding and stock pens for ranches in the west sector of the park. The station was named for an owner of the 63 Ranch.

The CM soon beyond Haver began the gradual and roundabout climb out of the park to Trout Creek Pass. On a two per cent grade it ascended the southeast side of the pass and crossed over the DSP&P tracks at the top. Just beyond this overpass was the South Park's Hilltop station. Shortly after the CM was built, the South Park changed the station name to Summit, and the CM adopted the name of Bath for its station. The Midland had a telegraph office, section house, bunkhouse, and siding there. It was a shipping point for a small quantity of lumber and cattle.

The Midland, like the South Park, had a history of changing ownership. It was in and out of receivership a number of times and was owned at different times by the Santa Fe, the C&S and Rio Grande Western (at the time that the rival D&RG got control of the RGW, the C&S was running all of them—including the South Park), and finally the Burlington. In 1917 A. E. Carlton bought the line and vigorously began improving the road. On Trout Creek Pass, for instance, the old sixty-pound rail was replaced with ninety-pound from Haver to Newett, a few miles down the west side, as part of his program. But World War I spawned government control of the railroads with the result that all through traffic was assigned to the D&RG. The Midland was finished. In late summer of 1918 passenger and freight service stopped, and the line was dismantled in 1921.

After abandonment, the highway over Wilkerson Pass was rerouted onto the Midland grade through Elevenmile Canyon and into the park. However, the road moved back onto the pass in 1931 when Denver built the Elevenmile Canyon dam and reservoir.

The demise of the Colorado Midland did not dramatically change South Park. Most of the passenger traffic, other than excursionists of an earlier day, had been headed straight through on luxury equipment to Leadville, Aspen, the resort of Glenwood Springs, or even the West Coast by connecting trains from Salt

Lake City. Freight primarily was coal, limestone, fruit, and cattle from the Western Slope. The CM did haul a tremendous tonnage of hay out of the park, but this shipping still could be handled by the Denver and South Park from Garo or Jefferson. By the time that the South Park also was abandoned, most of the local ranches, as well as the mines and other businesses, were shipping by truck.

Railroad buffs have a hard time accepting the fact that the railroads were no longer needed, though they had, indeed, once performed a necessary and resourceful service. But the people of South Park no longer depended on or supported the railroads. The same whistle of a steam engine which brings nostalgic memories and dreams of adventure to one person, meant, to another, grass fires and sooty curtains in the train's wake.

Requiescat in pace.

CHAPTER NINE

The Salt Works

A unique chapter in South Park's early history was that of the salt works near Antero Junction. A square chimney, nestling between the hills northeast of the junction, still can be seen at the site where salt was being produced a century ago.

The works were built at a spring near Salt Creek. The salts found in the area around Antero Reservoir existed originally in a salt sea of the Pennsylvanian Age in geological time. They now seep up in alkaline marshes of the area, and a small saline pond called Salt Lake existed in the early days where the reservoir now lies. The compound in the Salt Spring was sodium chloride. Although there is another salt spring about four miles northwest of the salt works, the spring at the works was more heavily mineralized and was the better known.

In the area of the spring, herds of buffalo and antelope had gathered, attracting in turn bands of Utes who hunted and camped there frequently. The Indians found this gathering place of animals a fine hunting area but used the salt, too.

With the arrival of the earliest prospectors who crossed South Park, the salt spring had become familiar to the new settlers; Augusta Tabor mentioned in 1860 camping at the saline spring which proved to be unfit either for their use or for their stock's.

As early as November, 1861, commercial use of the salt was attempted. At that time J. C. Fuller ordered boilers and other equipment and began to advertise the salt from the spring as being fit for table use. He sold some of his "Pike's Peak Salt" to the miners in the region.

In the following year Charles Hall homesteaded the Salt Works Ranch. The story is that Hall passed through the park with a party and camped near the salt spring. Making coffee from what was thought to be ordinary water, Hall thought that someone in the group was playing jokes. After they discovered the real cause of the unpalatable brew, they went in search of better water and located the excellent Buffalo Spring nearby to the west. The Halls then decided to settle there.

Charles Hall, born in New York State but raised in Iowa, came to Colorado in 1858. In 1859 he went to California Gulch where he had some success in prospecting. Two years later he and two companions went prospecting in the San Juan Mountains but became lost and nearly starved to death. Hall, suspecting that his companions were considering him as their most likely food supply, removed himself hastily and made his way alone to Baker's Park, the site of Silverton. When he arrived there, he weighed only forty-eight pounds; but he was nursed back to health by Mary Nye, a woman with two children who had joined the miners there after she was deserted by her husband. Charles and Mary were married in 1862 shortly before their arrival at the salt springs.

The original ranchhouse was a log cabin which later was incorporated into the frame house at the Salt Springs Ranch. Fuller evidently having abandoned his enterprise, Hall manufactured some salt in 1862 and 1863.

Indians still frequented the area. When Hall tried to sell them the salt which they felt was their own in the first place, the Indians refused to buy. They protested to the government, and Hall ultimately was compelled to give a certain amount of salt annually to the Indians.

At times Mary Hall was alone at the ranch when the Indians came around. Once when they seemed to be threatening her, Mary stood her ground with a butcher knife. The chief of the band was so impressed with her spirit that he later tried to trade a squaw to Hall in exchange for Mary.

In 1864 the Colorado Salt Works was organized with Hall being one of the incorporators as well as the supervisor of the works. With Hall in the enterprise was John Quincy Adams Rollins, for whom Rollinsville, Colorado, and Rollins Pass are named. Rollins had come to Denver in 1860 and shortly thereafter prospected in Boulder County. He next went to Buckskin Joe, where he was an investor in the rich Phillips Lode.

Rollins put at least $40,000 of his mining profits into the salt works, while Hall and a Mr. Lane invested another $20,000 in the plant. A mason from the Arkansas Valley was hired to build the sixty-foot high chimney. The building, which is still standing, was an ell-shaped, frame structure, 160 by 70 feet long and three stories high. Eighteen iron evaporating kettles—three inches thick, forty inches across, and about a foot and a half deep—were brought in from Missouri by ox team at a cost of $1,500 each. The partially evaporated brine ran from these kettles into two pans, eleven by twenty-eight feet in size, for further evaporation and separation. Then the purer brine went into six smaller pans for a final processing. Anywhere from six to fourteen men worked at the plant at a time.

The principal use of the salt was in chloridizing ore, although some was used for ranching and domestic purposes, too. The mines used cheaper, less pure salt than did the others. Much of the salt went to the refinery at the Whale Mine across Kenosha Pass in Hall Valley, where Charles Hall was an investor. Some of it also was shipped over the Park Range at $60 a ton to Georgetown, a figure which was low enough to compete with Eastern salt for use in the mines.

When salt from the works first was sold in Denver in 1864 for $4.50 a pound, the *Rocky Mountain News* had exclaimed, "What are the salt works doing?" The major problem seems to have been expenditures for new equipment at this time. Within a year the price was down to $1.00 per pound at a competitive bulk rate.

The salt works and the Hall ranch became a center of activity for the portion of South Park surrounding them. As travelers came and went over either Trout Creek or Weston Pass, they often stopped at the ranch. Bayard Taylor's entourage stopped there in 1866 with newspaperman Byers and several others. They were on their way from Buckskin Joe and the California Gulch areas to Canon City in connection with Taylor's lecture tour.

He reported that there were herds of cattle around the salt works, and a number of cabins had been built. The party, with two other men who came in later, sat around the stove congenially while Mrs. Hall quickly prepared a large supper for the houseful of unexpected guests. They all spent the night, too. Taylor pronounced afterward, "The life of a settler in Colorado necessarily entails these duties, and if they are always so cheerfully and kindly performed as in our case, the Territory may be proud of its citizens."

Because it was raining, Taylor made no effort to see the salt works. Anyway, as he said, "We all know . . . that a salt spring is like any other spring, except as to taste." He added that the salt was being produced successfully despite high costs of labor, supplies, and fuel.

During the following winter Father Dyer reported staying there. At the time he was on his way to the Arkansas River from Fairplay, but the sun on the snow was so intensely bright that he had to stop at the ranch to prevent snow blindness. While he was there, he held services, which were attended by the local cowboys and Indians, miners and mule skinners.

The salt works operated successfully only through 1867, when a legal action arose over the ownership of the land. Apparently, when the land first was homesteaded by Hall, a prior claim—perhaps Fuller's—had been easily settled because the alkaline land seemed worthless. The law suit brought in 1867 attempted to prove that the homestead was not being used for agricultural purposes but for minerals—a claim which was easily disproved by the cattle being run there. By the time that the case was settled, however, the salt works had incurred so much legal expense that it was in financial trouble. Furthermore, the railroads had made it possible for salt suppliers from the East to seize the better part of the market at the mines.

An additional problem was that the springs themselves were

not sufficiently saline. The Hayden report of 1869 noted, "The springs are two in number, but the brine is not abundant or strong." Since fuel for evaporating had to be hauled some little distance, the weakness of the brine pushed the evaporating costs too high. Rollins and Hall in an effort to cut costs, had even been forced to put in an artesian well beside the salt works in an effort to bring in stronger brine and to eliminate pumping the water.

The Halls continued to live at the Salt Works Ranch even after production stopped in 1869. Not only did travelers continue to come there as a matter of convenience, but also the ranch was a warm haven in cases of emergency. Charles Nachtrieb from the Arkansas Valley was bringing supplies from Denver to California Gulch on three wagons during the winter of 1870. He was caught in such a blizzard in South Park that he had to take refuge at the ranch. His oxen died there, and Charlie could not get the supplies to California Gulch where food was running out. Finally volunteers came over to the Salt Works Ranch from the Gulch and took back enough food by snowshoe.

And in January of 1875 Judge Elias Dyer, Father Dyer's son, stopped at the ranch in his flight from the Arkansas Valley to Fairplay during the Gas Creek War. The Judge had been run out of his district by a mob of about seventy-five vigilantes who disagreed with the Judge's opinion on the innocence of one Elijah Gibbs, accused of murder in the war there between sheep and cattle interests. After Judge Dyer left the Salt Works Ranch, he was stopped and intimidated again by the mob before he reached Fairplay. In July the Judge was shot at Granite after his deputy had arrested the leaders of the mob.

On the whole, the Hall ranch was the scene of a calmer life. The Halls were prosperous and well known. Mrs. Hall became the proud possessor in 1867 of the first sewing machine in the region—even before Mrs. Myers of Montgomery acquired hers! Mrs. Hall kept a fine herd of dairy cows, and an overnight visitor to the ranch in 1871 reported seeing 100 pans of milk, covered over with the richest of cream, and two or three kegs of luscious butter. The icy spring water was allowed to run through the dairy house for refrigeration.

Mary Hall was evidently a many-sided person as well as an industrious one. In the summer of 1872 a distinguished group of "Little Londoners" from Colorado Springs stopped at the ranch during a mountain excursion. This party included, among others, General Palmer, president of the Denver and Rio Grande Railway, with Mrs. Palmer; Governor A. C. Hunt; and authors Grace Greenwood and Eliza Greatorix. Eliza was particularly impressed by Mrs. Hall's outstanding collection of minerals.

During these years at the salt works, Hall served in the Territorial Legislature for three terms. The family left the ranch in 1878, joining the rush to Leadville. However, Hall did not go as an ordinary prospector but as a contractor. He built the streets of the new town and later organized the gas and electric companies there as well as in Pueblo. In 1880 Charles Hall became a partner with H. A. W. Tabor and Bill Bush in building the famous Windsor Hotel in Denver, although Hall shortly sold his interest to Augusta Tabor.

Hall subsequently developed mining interests around Breckenridge, Leadville, the San Juans, and even Arizona. He died in 1907.

In 1881 another group of investors, known as the Colorado Salt Works Manufacturing Company, sank a thousand-foot well in an effort to get stronger brine for the works. This new group included J. Alden Smith, Frank Hall, Leander Brink, and H. P. Lyon, the last being the manager. They hoped that the proximity of the works to the new Denver and South Park Railway would make it possible to market the salt profitably. However, after evaporating a good quantity of salt for a year or so, this company also gave up in 1883, and the works have remained idle since.

The ranch continued to operate. Mail was delivered at Buffalo Springs for the fifty people reportedly living at the Salt Works in 1884, although this figure must have included the neighboring ranches as well.

The Charles Hall family still owned the ranch at the salt works. Charles and Mary had had three children—Minnie, Charles, Jr., and Mildred. Mildred, who took up the ranch in later years, was born at the Ellis Ranch on the Turkey Creek toll road. Following an exclusive education at Wolfe Hall in Denver and at Wellesley College, she studied dramatics in the East. However, she suddenly gave up her theatrical career and returned to the Salt Works Ranch, at the time being married to a Mr. Wessells.

While Mildred had been gone, the neighboring JP Ranch had been purchased by Thomas McQuaid. Tom McQuaid was the son of "Barnie" (Bernard) and Delia McQuaid, who had left Massachusetts in 1860 to go to California by way of Cape Horn. In California's mining country Tom was born. The family came to California Gulch in 1870. As Tom grew up, he became a cow puncher in the Salida area.

In 1911 Mildred Hall Wessells and Tom McQuaid married, a wedding which would seem to have brought together a mismatched pair if ever there was one. However, it was a notably successful marriage. The pair built up their holdings to a total of seven ranches, and they owned or leased some 20,000 acres of South Park's rich range land. They ran about 10,000 head of cattle carrying fourteen brands. Mildred died in 1945, and the rough, tough, indomitable Tom died in 1965.

The old salt works chimney is a landmark for a unique activity in South Park's history while the Salt Works Ranch is a landmark for a family prominent in an important phase of the park's life—ranching.

CHAPTER TEN

The Bountiful Ranch Land

High in the Rocky Mountain upland, South Park has a short summer and growing season. Winter temperatures drop to twenty-five degrees below zero on occasion, and seldom do summer temperatures go above eighty degrees. Despite an abundance of water flowing across the park from the surrounding mountains, the mean precipitation is only about thirteen and a half inches. South Park is high and cool, but it is a semi-arid land. It is not a country for gardens, but it is a land of lush hay fields and cattle and sheep ranges.

Ranching was undertaken within a year or two after the first gold strikes. By 1861 the first ditch rights for agricultural purposes had been recorded. However, farming as such was not attempted. Food supplies like corn, potatoes, onions, and cabbage were shipped in to the mining settlements from farms along the Arkansas of the Huerfano region.

Nevertheless, when Nathan C. Meeker came to Colorado in 1869 to report on the agricultural possibilities of the territory for the New York *Tribune,* he was greatly impressed with South Park's fertility and climate—so much so, in fact, that he enthusiastically determined to establish an agricultural colony in the section of the park around today's Elevenmile Canyon Reservoir.

His plan was to bring fifty or sixty families to the area to undertake irrigated farming. However, one of the members of Meeker's party on the tour was William N. Byers, editor of the *Rocky*

Mountain News, and formerly a correspondent to that journal from South Park. Byers corrected the New Yorker's impressions of South Park's climate with the result that Meeker shifted the location of his colony to the site of Greeley.

The Hayden Survey more accurately than Meeker observed that the park had about 700 square miles of excellent grazing land. The report also noted that another 174 square miles, principally in the northwestern part of the basin, would be cultivatable.

These observations, however, were theorizing on a *fait accompli,* for South Park by 1870 had become a great open range for some 6,000 head of cattle and 700 head of horses. And Fairplay was already as much a ranch center as a mining one.

But just when South Park and Colorado in general were suffering from the effects of the financial Panic of 1873, a plague of locusts also devastated the range land in 1874. Then another wave of the grasshoppers descended in 1876. The cattle and hay industries recovered, and the park soon was known as one of the principal hay producing regions of the state. In 1905 the Colorado Midland shipped 100 cars of hay out of Hartsel alone.

With the water from the Platte and the Tarryall drainages, more than seventy-five per cent of the ranches were irrigated. By 1883 there were nearly 50,000 head of cattle, 5,000 head of horses, and 10,000 sheep in the park.

The cattle ranchers in the area soon organized the Park County Cattle Growers' Association, which later merged with Fremont County's organization to become the largest in the state. The cattle associations filled a need much as the early mining districts had. The ranchers also cooperated in semi-annual roundups on the open range. Rather than shipping their cattle to market for sale, the ranchers sold their cattle at the roundups to buyers who came up to the park for the purpose.

Because of its location South Park was not on the usual routes of long cattle drives. However, a good-sized herd occasionally moved through on its way to northwestern Colorado.

The kind of trouble which arose in other regions between cattlemen and sheepmen, especially in the Salida and Buena Vista

215

districts, was largely avoided in South Park because sheep were not grazed on the open range there with few exceptions. Sheep were introduced for the most part when ranches were sold, the sheep then being grazed on private land.

In the 1890's the United States Government became concerned about the free use of the public domain by stock growers and about damage to watersheds. Forest reserves were created, and interests using the reserves for grazing were assessed fees. Cattlemen in South Park took part in a vigorous fight which Colorado ranchers, with the support of the governor and leading newspapers, waged against the government action. The result in South Park was that the ranchers succeeded in confining the new grazing districts primarily to mountainous forest land.

In 1905 the Forest Service was created, and in 1907 the former reserves became national forests. Today most of the mountain land surrounding South Park lies within the boundaries of Pike National Forest. It is maintained for "multiple use"—that is, the Forest Service permits and controls use of the forest for grazing, mining, water supplies, and recreation. In present times the heaviest use, in terms of human activity, has come to be for recreation. Eighteen campgrounds are available for outdoorsmen, especially fishermen.

However, the foremost concern of the Forest Service is the protection of watersheds. The seemingly abundant surface water of South Park is all spoken for, even before the sparkling snows on the mountain peaks begin to melt, and the system by which it is claimed greatly affects the development of the park.

Most of the earliest miners and ranchers in Colorado came from parts of the country where there was plenty of water—enough to permit a "riparian" system of use. A man's land included a stream of some sort almost always, and he simply took what water he needed as it passed his stream banks.

In Colorado, and South Park, there were not enough streams to flow through each parcel of land. In the early 1860's a system was established by the territorial legislature which permitted non-riparian landowners, those without access to a stream, the right to appropriate and divert water to their land. The rights were based on the priority of their claims, or prior appropriation. These water rights have been an important element in the development of South Park's ranches from the earliest years.

Turning to the history of individual ranches, any account of ranching in South Park must begin chronologically with Sam Hartsel and end with the immense spread which grew out of his Hartsel Ranch. Sam Hartsel was there first, and his ranch grew steadily under his management but fantastically later under the management of others to a holding of more than 200,000 acres.

Hartsel was born in Bucks County, Pennsylvania, in 1836. As a gangling, six-foot-tall lad of eighteen, he began to herd cattle to New York. Then in 1857 he went to Iowa and from there to Kansas, where he worked for Russell, Majors, and Waddell. He came to the Tarryall district in Colorado in 1860.

At Tarryall he gave up prospecting after just a few weeks and began herding cattle for Bowers and Warren of Hamilton. Actually, the herds under his care were merely worn-out, footsore oxen which had hauled wagons across the plains. Nevertheless, they were all that was to be had for "domestic beef." Soon he was buying these sorry specimens for ten or twenty dollars, fattening them up, and selling them for ninety or a hundred dollars to the local butchers. He grazed the animals on his Pennsylvania Ranch, three miles below Tarryall.

When Duke Green and Ed Shook herded twenty top-quality Shorthorn cows (with a couple of registered animals among them) to Colorado from Iowa in 1861, Hartsel bought them up. With this stock as a beginning, Hartsel relocated his ranch in 1862, homesteading 160 acres at the junction of the South and Middle forks of the South Platte River.

Encouraged with the success of this small herd, Hartsel went to Missouri in 1864 to purchase a herd of purebred Shorthorns— 148 cows and two bulls—two-thirds of the herd being all white. The cattle were ferried across the Missouri River to Kansas where they were wintered. About a half a dozen of them were killed there by Indians. The next summer Hartsel and his Mexican cowpunchers got the cattle west as far as Bent's Fort. He left the herd near there while he went on to South Park for the winter

217

of 1865-66. In the summer of 1866 he succeeded in bringing the stock on into the park. There he had just about all of South Park at his disposal for open range without fear of crossbreeding of this herd with other cattle. The cattle thrived so well that Hartsel was selling both beef and breeding animals within a few years.

Hartsel brought his first horses to the park in 1869 from Illinois and began to raise them, too. He broke young colts by putting them on a hay rake.

During his first years in South Park, Hartsel built a sawmill, a trading post, wagon shop, and blacksmith shop at the site of the town of Hartsel. The various businesses were well located since they were at the crossroads of the heavily used trails across the park from Wilkerson Pass and Currant Creek Pass. The wagon shop, which employed some of the best wagon makers in the West, became famous.

Hartsel was joined in South Park by a brother who later disappeared. The brother was not found for several years, when his skeleton and that of his horse were found under a tree where they had been struck by lightning.

Located near the popular Indian springs, Hartsel's trading post attracted many Utes, with whom Hartsel was on good terms. The Utes made regular seasonal visits to the hot springs to ease their winter's stiffness and the aches from their joints.

There is a story that one day out in the park Hartsel was approached by what he took to be a band of friendly Utes. Instead, they were unfriendly Cheyennes who took him captive. While Hartsel was in their hands, the Cheyennes found a small band of Utes and killed some of them, taking others captive. After Hartsel agreed to guide the Cheyennes to the trail to Ute Pass, he was released.

The hot springs were developed by Hartsel in addition to his other enterprises. So as to have some of the therapeutic mineral water for his own use, he laid a wooden pipe from the springs to his house, two miles to the east. The pipe was made of six-foot lengths of log, about nine inches in diameter, with a small, round bore through the center. The water was pumped through the pipe by a wheel which is still seen near the abandoned railroad grade at Hartsel.

The temperature of the water, 134 degrees F, soon attracted travelers on the main routes across the park. What a joy the hot baths must have been to dust-caked freighters from the long wagon trains that were passing through to the San Juans or Leadville! While the blacksmiths and wagon makers did repairs, the mule skinners reveled at the baths. Although there are two other springs near the town, both of these are cold and so were not developed.

Sometime in the late 1870's Hartsel also built a hotel across the river from the spring. In July, 1879, the hotel was described in a newspaper as being a "well-kept house, largely patronized." At the time it was leased to a John Wisentine. The news article went on to predict that if the D&RG built through Hartsel, the resort would be even more popular. The guests at that time were passengers from the busy stage lines.

However, despite the ranch, the junction of two main roads, the hot spring, and the hotel, the town is reported to have had a permanent population of only five in 1880, a figure which scarcely seems correct. There also was a post office at the time.

After the Colorado Midland was built in the 1880's, Hartsel and its hotel and springs were publicized by the railroad. The hotel was still a small structure which accommodated only twenty, and room rates were ten dollars a week. In later years wings were added to the first hotel. The central portion was a one-and-a-half story structure with dormer windows. The small yellow building which stands next to the present hotel was one of these wings. They were used for invalids who came to the springs since bedrooms in the main building were upstairs. The hotel taxied guests to the springs in a closed hansom carriage. The old hotel was replaced about 1900. It burned in the 1970's.

Hartsel was a bachelor until 1877 when the widow of Frank Mayol finally made a married man of him. She had two children whom he adopted, and the couple had a son and three daughters of their own. The son died in his youth. The family moved to Denver in later years, and Hartsel died there in 1918.

Not only was he remarkable in his enterprise but also his ranch was known for its generosity, especially to cowboys riding the "grubline." The family ranchhouse, which had replaced Hartsel's original log cabin, burned in 1958.

After Hartsel sold out and left the park, the hotel and the springs were owned and leased by a number of parties, the two properties often being under separate management. One of the hotel operators around the turn of the century was the widow of Chubb Newitt from Garo. E. W. Hanlin ran it after 1913 for a number of years.

The bathhouse which stands empty today was built in 1915. It replaced an earlier, more modest structure. There were indoor baths as well as an outdoor pool in its heyday.

The transfer of the properties at Hartsel is confusing at best. In 1908 the Townsite Company of St. Louis bought the hotel and the townsite separately from the ranch, the ranch having been sold in 1907 with the exception of the 240 acres around the springs. The ranch land at the time of sale totaled 8,709 acres. Purchasers were the South Park Land and Livestock Company, which had been organized in 1881 and had taken up large ranch holdings around the state. One of the incorporators was Lyman Robinson of Canon City, who had made a fortune at Leadville. J. D. Husted of Cripple Creek, who owned the company when the Hartsel Ranch was bought, also had other large ranches at Divide (the Crescent Ranch), Meeker, the Grand Valley, and elsewhere. Most of Husted's enterprises were put together with capital from assorted subscribers, including Eastern college professors and clergymen from Boston. The South Park Land and Livestock Company sold the ranch within a very few years to Swift and Company, meat packers.

In the meantime, the townsite company was sold to the Snyder Company, and that holder also was bought out by Swift and Company. Swift then operated a little kingdom of its own until 1916 when the government broke it up. In the interval Swift had built the South Park Mercantile store, operated for them by the Lockes. Locke bought the store from Swift in 1916, he and his two sons running it until 1965 when it was sold to personable Ray Moore. One of the Locke brothers, George, was a Colorado state senator.

Gene Kleinknecht, who had a store, the hotel, the bathhouse, and a garage at various times, also had the townsite company. The town's population is about fifty.

The schoolhouse at Hartsel first stood on the ranch property about a block from its present location. It was moved into town after a survey revealed the original error. The school was used before the turn of the century primarily for short terms "to hold the district." Among its teachers were Mrs. E. W. Hanlin and Alice McLaughlin Wonder of Fairplay, who "held" many a district for South Park in the early years.

In 1944 Swift and Company sold the Hartsel Ranch to Roach of Houston, who in turn sold to A. T. "Cap" McDannald in 1946. McDannald, head of the McDannald Oil Company, also acquired the 10,000-acre Ken Caryl Ranch at the old site of Bradford near Denver in 1949. This ranch was used for holding and fattening cattle for the Denver market.

The Hartsel Ranch was only 10,000 acres when McDannald acquired it, but he built it to over 200,000 acres in the next fifteen years, mostly through outright purchases of land but also through leasing of private and government acreage. He ran a large number of sheep as well as cattle with sheep-grazing permits extending as far north as Georgetown. In 1953 he sold 1300 head of purebred cattle in Denver for $400,000, reportedly the largest private sale of registered cattle in America.

During the 1950's McDannald did some oil well drilling south of Hartsel. The Shell Oil Company also sank six wells east of Hartsel in 1956. However, neither these wells nor some drilled north of town in the 1930's yielded anything.

In 1959 McDannald sold about half of the Hartsel Ranch to Estates of the World, Inc., an organization incorporated in Hawaii but having a number of Denver investors. This group attempted for a time to promote a subdivision of 10,000 five-acre ranch tracts without notable success. McDannald died in 1963. In 1966 the remaining 100,000 acres sold for about $2,000,000 to two groups of purchasers, the Badger Grazing Association and the Eleven Mile Grazing Association.

A herd of about 1,000 antelope roam the vast Hartsel ranch, mingling with cattle and, at one time, fenced buffalo—reminders of the *Bayou Salado* which Sam Hartsel homesteaded little more than a century ago.

A neighboring ranch, the Santa Maria Ranch about three miles north of Hartsel, consists of about 12,000 acres, 1,100 of which are irrigated. The ranch has some of the best water rights on the South Platte. The ranch originally was owned by Adolphus Fehringer, who sold in 1879 to Hal Chalmers from London, England. Chalmers built the ranch up into the Chalmers-Galloway Livestock Company. The ranch, later operated by his son, was sold in 1945. Owned first by Texans and then by a Mexican cattle corporation, the property now is combined with the McDowell Ranch (the old Adolph Guiraud property) just through the water gap in Red Hill.

The land east of the Santa Maria Ranch is part of the old Elkhorn Ranch. The ranches in this part of the park, now taken up in the Hartsel Ranch for the most part, are bounded by the Puma Hills and Badger Mountain with its fire lookout station and microwave tower. North of Badger Mountain lies La Salle Pass with a country road which connects the ranch country of the park with the lower Tarryall region. La Salle Pass took its name from a pioneer rancher in the Tarryall. South of Badger Mountain is Wilkerson Pass, a paved highway since 1938, which also bears the name of a pioneer rancher.

A few miles down the highway to the west of Wilkerson Pass the crossroad called Glentivar is now deserted. Its main function was as a post office for the twenty or thirty ranches of the La Salle Pass and Sulphur Mountain regions. At one time the old Colorado City wagon road was about a mile farther south than U.S. 24 now is, and Glentivar's location accordingly was to the south, too. At the former place there were about six large buildings and a few smaller houses. By the 1930's its population was only eight, however.

One of the early ranches in this section of the park belonged to Joseph Rogers, a French-Canadian. Located south of Glentivar in the Elevenmile Canyon Reservoir area, the ranch is now under water.

Rogers came to South Park from Denver in 1873. He built his operation into a large ranch, running about 13,000 sheep. In addition to the ranch near the reservoir, he also had property on the western side of the park below Weston Pass. Rogers, the prototype of rugged individualism, was said to carry guns at all times and to use them when necessary. Although cattle were not usually his target, he claimed that he shot the last eight Texas longhorns in the region down near Dick's Peak.

Joseph Rogers died in 1924. His wife lived in Colorado Springs in later years although the City of Denver had given her permission to continue living at the ranchhouse after the reservoir was built in 1931.

South of the Rogers ranch was the Epperson place. In his story of South Park ranching episodes, Harry Epperson, the son of the homesteader, has given a vivid picture of life around Howbert. The Eppersons came to the area in 1887.

The *Colorado Graphic* of December 17, 1887, says that Howbert was then petitioning for a post office. The article also says that Howbert had previously been called Dell's Camp. The place got its post office, which was combined with Dell's grocery store, and in time there were also a drugstore, butcher shop, hotel, two saloons, sawmill, and the depot. Twenty-five houses sprang up around the railroad station, and Howbert had two ladies of the night but no school. The Eppersons had to move to Colorado City in the winter so that the children could learn their reading and writing.

Epperson recalls the wager that J. B. Sims, who had a ranch southwest of Howbert, and Joe Rogers made on the outcome of the 1892 Presidential race. Rogers lost and had to put on an all-day shindig for the neighborhood in payment. People came from miles around for the barbecue, which was handled by the local barber. In addition, there was a horse race with entries brought in from as far away as Denver. And finally there was a dance, held in the hall above Dell's store. (Dell's family, according to Epperson, was a self-contained entertainment troupe—all being musicians and having a son-in-law who was a square dance caller besides. The Dell home was on Currant Creek Pass, where they operated a sawmill.)

Sims was a prominent rancher and captain of the big semi-annual roundups. These were held in the spring and fall and covered an enormous range encompassing Park, Chaffee, Fremont, and Teller counties.

Southeast from the Howbert area, roads extended back into the ranching and lumbering areas around Thirtynine Mile Mountain, Guffey, Oil Creek, and Cripple Creek; into the Lone Chimney ranches east of the Elevenmile area; and northeast toward Florissant. George Frost, formerly a manufacturer from Boston, had an extensive ranch in the Lone Chimney area, built Lake George, and established the town there.

In the early days the stage station and post office in the area of Lake George was called Rocky. It was a settlement of about twenty-five residents near the present junction of the two gravel roads which lead to the reservoir and to Wilkerson Pass via the back route. Rocky, although not in South Park, was the post office for the earliest ranches in the southern part of the valley. The old road came from Rocky over Wilkerson Pass with a stage station on the pass called Illinois House. Illinois House was still in existence in 1898.

The next stage station beyond Illinois House was the Sulphur Spring, and at least as early as 1880 Sulphur Spring was also the jumping-off place for the road over La Salle Pass to Bordenville to the north. Originally called Eagle Sulphur Spring, the station was later called Oliver Hot Springs for many years.

At the spring there was a log ranchhouse. One early traveler who reported stopping there was invited by the owner to walk back to the spring to have a drink, but "a fearful smell greeted our nasal organs. I instantly concluded that there was some defect in the sewerage of the place." Nevertheless, he tasted the spring water. He then commented, "I thought I had smelt and tasted sulphur water before, but [this] was on the basis of homeopathy run mad."

224

The Salt Works, photographed in the 1870's, was built in 1864. For the few years that it operated successfully, much of its product went to ore refineries. *Abby Kernochan collection.*

Samuel Hartsel, one of the first ranchers in South Park, established the Hartsel Ranch with its pure-bred herd, the town of Hartsel, and the hotel and original bath-house there. *Courtesy of the Denver Public Library Western Collection.*

Resourceful Sam Hartsel used this water wheel to pump mineral water from the hot springs to his ranch house, two miles away, through a pipe made of bored logs.

226

The town of Hartsel in about 1900 consisted mostly of the Midland depot, the new hotel and the hot springs bathhouse (in the foreground), a general store, and the schoolhouse. *Courtesy of the Denver Public Library Western Collection, L. C. McClure photo.*

The large section of the Hotel Hartsel was new when this photograph was taken. The story-and-a-half section to the left was the original hotel, and the low portion beyond was an annex. The hotel carried its guests in a hansom to the springs across the river. *Courtesy of the Denver Public Library Western Collection, L. C. McClure photo.*

The Hartsel schoolhouse, where South Park's favorite teacher of long ago, Alice McLaughlin Wonder, "held the district."

The South Park Mercantile Company originally belonged to Swift and Company, the meat packers who owned the Hartsel Ranch, the town site, and the store at one time.

229

Mexican sheepherders in South Park have erected landmarks on many of the hills around south park.

A sheepherder carried timbers from a deserted ranch and quartz from a nearby Indian quarry to create this cross near County Road 53.

Kester was a post office on Currant Creek Pass. Behind the ghost town is Thirtynine Mile Mountain.

Little Black Mountain provides a backdrop to one of the few remaining buildings at Whitehorn, a mining town at the south end of the park.

The old Adolph Guiraud ranch was photographed from the site of the town of Garo which was situated across the Middle Fork of the South Platte River from the ranch. Guiraud homesteaded here in 1863. Mt. Silverheels and Trout Creek lie behind the house. *Courtesy of the Library, State Historical Society, William Smallwood photo.*

Now the McDowell Ranch, the Guiraud house has been extensively remodeled but is still standing.

The town of Garo has been demolished since this photograph was taken in fairly recent times. The store at the left once belonged to "Chubb" Newitt and later to the Turner family. It is still standing. The schoolhouse in the upper center is now at the South Park City restoration. *South Park City collection.*

The 63 Ranch near the Buffalo Springs is one of the oldest ranches in the park.

A hunter's rig rolls across Weston Pass while sheep graze unconcernedly, about 1900. *Beth Kraig collection.*

The McLaughlin stage arrives at Pearts' Ranch with a party who have come to celebrate a birthday, country style. *South Park City collection.*

Tarryall Creek meanders down the valley behind the old Borden place at Bordenville. The Bordenville post office was in the wing on the right side of the house, which was built in 1865.

Kenosha House was a stage station at the west side of Kenosha Hill. It was built in the early 1860's and was still operating in the late 1890's. This picture was taken about 1870. *Courtesy of the Library, State Historical Society of Colorado.*

The second schoolhouse at Jefferson.

The humps of the Buffalo Peaks gleam above the waters of Antero Reservoir, built in 1913 and now part of the Denver water system. *Courtesy of the Colorado Game, Fish, and Parks Department; George D. Andrews photo.*

Like an immense string of beads, pipe for Colorado Springs' water supply lies waiting to be buried in the Agate Creek area of South Park in 1965. *Colorado Springs Utilities Department photo.*

Sheep and cattle graze on the same range at the Hartsel Ranch.

Another harvest of gold, a crop of South Park hay, glistens in the autumn sun below the Buffalo Peaks.

The Sulphur Spring was located near a barren brown rise of ground to the southwest of Sulphur Mountain. Other than the unique odor of its environs, there was nothing to distinguish the place. Nevertheless, the Colorado Midland Railway was very interested in it and publicized in the 1890's that it had been purchased by "Boston and Denver investors" and named the Colorado White Sulphur Springs, "to distinguish it from the White Sulphur Springs of Virginia." The investors planned to erect a "commodious hotel" with two stories and a broad veranda, as well as a bathhouse. They also thought that, since the proposed site for the hotel was level, it would be "admirably adapted for fine carriage drives"—that being the most practical aspect of the entire plan. Despite the Midland's encouragement, a spa never was built and the spring became a cattle wallow instead.

The spring was near Ben Spinney's ranch, which abutted the Rogers Ranch and ran westward along the Platte. The Midland had a station at Spinney; and H. C. Gill, who operated sawmills all along the right of way, put up a mill at Spinney in 1890.

Next to the Spinney ranch on the west was the Jerome Harrington ranch. The Harrington's homesteaded in the early 1870's and gradually built up a 6,000-acre spread. Jerome Harrington was from New York State, and Mrs. Harrington, from Maine, was the sister of Ben Spinney. This family was typical of Eastern farmers who took up ranches throughout South Park, especially along the Platte. These Easterners lent a distinct character of industry and permanence to their ranches.

The Harrington ranch was taken over eventually by their daughter and her husband, A. A. Buckley. Their ranch, which originally had raised cattle and horses, then turned to sheep raising. In spring Mexican families from Taos, New Mexico, came onto the ranch to assist with lambing and shearing.

Reminders of Mexican sheepherders in South Park are often found in the park. The sheepherders whiled away the hours and day by building cairns of rock or sometimes by propping up gnarled pieces of wood as sentinels. Sometimes they even built fairly elaborate crucifixes. One such wooden cross with two arms can be seen near a large stone cairn on a high, wooded hill west of U.S. 285 near the Buffalo Peaks. A unique cross was laid out on a hillside south of Hartsel. Here a framework of lumber was placed on the ground and was then filled with chips of white quartz. The white chips, interestingly, had been gathered from a nearby Indian quarry where quartz boulders had years before been broken down and flaked for the making of points.

The portion of the park lying south and west of the Agate Creek area has a history quite unlike the rest of the ranches of the park. The hilly, secluded land around Black Mountain harbored a breed more akin to the rough, tough cattle days of the TV Westerns.

In the Buffalo Slough country around Balfour there occurred the one serious incident of feuding between cattlemen and sheepmen in South Park. Obe Fife, a cattleman, killed a sheep raiser named Scribner in a dispute over the use of the range. Partially to blame for the difficulty was the fact that there were so few fences—only natural boundaries such as rivers or mountain elevations.

On one occasion in 1885 the cattle ranchers cooperated in building a drift fence about thirty miles long from Pikes Peak out into South Park, but such a fence was not helpful in keeping herds separated. Cattle from the Chaffee County range also wandered over the mountains and mixed with Park and Fremont County herds. In 1883 rustling and changing of brands created hot feelings among the Black Mountain ranchers and those of the Arkansas River region. The murder of rancher Ed Watkins of Salida in that year touched off bad feeling that existed for ten years throughout the area. The IM Ranch on Badger Creek near Black Mountain was the center of much of the trouble.

Ira Mulock had taken up the IM around 1872 and soon was selling cattle to the mining towns in South Park and to settlements on the Arkansas. Mulock had an attraction for trouble. Once when he thought that he was not getting his fair share out of the cooperative roundup, he set up his own for a few years. For this undertaking he bought a yellow circus wagon and a "big top" to use as headquarters. Any self-respecting cowboy would have been sufficiently embarrassed by this outfit, but Mulock went too far by bringing in a bunch of mares for them to ride in the roundup. At that, the cowboys stampeded the offensive beasts into an arroyo by tying hides to their tails.

By 1883 Mulock and his three sons were running about 8,000 head of cattle, and Mulock was again taking part in the regular roundup with such ranchers from the Black Mountain district as William Gribble, the Eddy brothers, John Sweet, the Witchers, the Sampsons, the Gardners, and Freeman Waugh. At their roundup in Gribble Park, John Hyssong, a young cowboy working for Mulock, reported that a number of the Mulock brands had been changed to Ed Watkins' brand.

Twenty of the cowmen armed themselves and ran off about a hundred steers from Watkins' land as retribution. The cattle first were taken to the IM Ranch and then to the Robbins ranch near J. B. Sims' at Howbert. Both the South Park ranchers and Watkins were arrested the next day. The following day Watkins was found hanged in Canon City. When a group of South Park men went down to Salida for a hearing later on, a mob was waiting for them, so the ranchers promptly boarded the train again and left town.

The final outcome of the investigations was that almost all of Watkins' cattle were discovered to bear brands which had been changed. No one ever tried to repossess the cattle which had been run off the Watkins place by the South Park ranchers.

Mulock, however, figured in another unpleasant chapter of Park County history. Mulock had invested his cattle money in buying a bank in Canon City. At the time, George Green owned the 63 Ranch. (A small lake in a volcanic cone north of Antero Reservoir was called Green Lake.) Green sold the 63 Ranch to Haver, who owned the Cleveland Cattle Company, for $50,000. Then Green put his money in Mulock's bank. The bank failed, and, when the local investors suggested a fate for Mulock similar to that meted out previously to Ed Watkins, Mulock departed for Mexico. Green later is supposed to have gone to the bank, to have held it up at gunpoint for the round sum of $50,000, and to have left the country also. Mulock's nephew A. R. Gaumer, who was the cashier of the bank, bought the IM at a sheriff's sale and ran it under the name of the Boston Land and Cattle Company.

William Berry, the freighter from Fairplay who had been in trouble for playing pranks with the United States mail, had a ranch called the JI on Currant Creek Pass near Thirtynine Mile Mountain. Just over the south edge of the pass was a post office at Kester, whose deserted log buildings are still standing.

A little farther south a road ran west up Thirtynine Mile Creek behind Black Mountain where two legendary episodes took place. In the early days there had been a town called Badger City in this district, but by 1900 it was gone and there was another location called Black Mountain City. At about that time Joe Beeler came to Black Mountain City from Kansas and opened a store and a post office which he called Divine. He also had a lumber mill and a mine. The family, which included Mrs. Beeler, a son Harry, and a daughter Beulah, seemed to be a refined sort.

However, business was not good, and one day Harry was found butchering stolen calves which he intended to sell at Cripple Creek. Harry was sent to the penitentiary at Canon City where he went insane and subsequently was sent to the State Hospital at Pueblo. Mrs. Beeler obtained Harry's release to her custody and took him home to Black Mountain, unknown to the neighbors.

Mrs. Beeler lived there in poverty for a number of years after her husband died. After marrying three times, Beulah returned to the home on Black Mountain to live with her mother. During this time John Hyssong from the IM stopped occasionally to take care of supplies which the women seemed to need. Still no one had ever seen Harry, although rumors circulated for years that strange noises coming from the cabin belonged to the insane man.

Finally around 1930, when Beulah was dying in the Salida hospital, she revealed that Harry had been at the cabin in chains all that time. The Park County sheriff went down from Fairplay and found him bound, naked, filthy, and starving. He was taken to Fairplay, where his long hair and beard and his maniacal countenance caused a public sensation. He was at long last returned to the State Hospital, where he died twelve years later.

The other Black Mountain legend is about the last of the grizzly bears in South Park. Old Mose, as he came to be known, preyed on cattle around Black Mountain for decades, and there was a standing reward out for him for thirty-five years. He is said to have killed 800 cattle. He also claimed at least one human victim, Jake Radcliff, a hunter who had settled in Fairplay in 1863. In 1884 Radcliff and two other hunters named Seymour and Cory went after Old Mose. After ten days of stalking him, Radcliff came upon the bear. Old Mose attacked Radcliff and mortally wounded him. Radcliff was taken to the IM. A rider went north to Platte Station for a doctor, who arrived in the middle of the night. When the doctor got there, the badly clawed Radcliff was taken to Fairplay, but he died en route. In 1903 the skeleton of a cowboy was found on Thirtynine Mile Mountain, and it was determined that he too had been one of Old Mose's victims.

In 1904 a bear hunter from Idaho came after the famous Mose. Together with a local rancher and their hunting dogs, they finally brought Old Mose to bay after two months. It took six shots then to kill him. When the carcass was cut up, it was discovered that nearly one hundred bullets had found their mark in the old rogue's body.

Returning to the cattle story, the VVN ranch, owned by the Eddy-Bissell Cattle Company, lay on the northwest side of Black Mountain. It was operated by the Eddy brothers and was one of the better known ranches in the south end of the park. Although the ranch actually owned only eight pre-empted acres, it had access to a large range on government land. In fact, since a rancher could fence any amount of government land so long as it was not enclosed, the Eddys had put up fencing on three sides of a good-sized piece of land and used Black Mountain as a natural barricade on the fourth, unfenced side.

The Eddys also grazed their cattle far from their home range. Some of their herds were put on range across Poncha, Monarch, and Marshall passes. Another herd grazed in lofty Taylor Park.

In addition to their routine cattle operation, the Eddys unknowingly got involved in some rustling, too. It developed that their trail herd foreman, Martin Morose, was collecting his own little herd of strays on the side. Morose left the territory after he was caught and set himself up in the rustling business with an organized gang in New Mexico and Mexico. He finally was killed by authorities in Texas, with the help of a former girlfriend.

Around the turn of the century many of the ranchers marketed and butchered at Whitehorn, one of today's ghost towns. Whitehorn, along with the Cameron Mountain mining camps of Manoa and Cameron, was active around the turn of the century. Today the country road to Salida passes Whitehorn and goes up Willow Creek to cross the ridge on the north side of Cameron Mountain.

The Cameron range, mountain, and town were named for Thomas Cameron, a pioneer of the Salida area. Cameron's wife was the sister of Sam Hartsel.

North of the rolling hills around Whitehorn and the Wagon Tongue Creek areas was a short-lived town called Trump. Set over near Kaufman Ridge, Trump was similar to Glentivar in that its main function seems to have been as a post office for neighboring ranches. There also was a store there at times. Trump appeared on maps in the 1930's, but its population was only three by 1936.

Another brief settlement was at Antelope Springs. The town there never developed very far, although remnants of a few cabins still are seen where the county road makes a sharp turn away from the springs themselves.

Just six miles southwest of Hartsel, the town of Salina existed around 1906 and 1907. In this area the Federal Government gave land to veterans after World War I, according to an old-timer; but they were unable to achieve any success with farm crops and left.

A postal directory in 1907 also listed Richards, which received its mail from Hartsel. Richards may have been only a ranch, though.

Northwest of Hartsel along Colorado 9 there are a number of ranches which date from the 1800's. The Badger Springs Ranch goes back at least to 1877. Until 1882 it belonged to Harry Epperson's family, who later lived at Howbert. At the Spring Ranch the Eppersons built bunkhouses and stables for wagon traffic on the road from Colorado City to Leadville. During the peak of the Leadville boom, the Eppersons made about a hundred dollars a day in board, lodging, and feed for stock.

Horace Alden and his father Elija bought up 560 acres below Garo in 1879. Originally from Canada, Alden was an industrious rancher who put in three miles of irrigation ditches as well as several artificial lakes. The ranchhouse, with its white clapboard siding and bay window, has more the aspect of an Eastern farm than a Western ranch. Alden was a commissioner for Park County and also a representative to the Colorado General Assembly. Elija Alden and Mrs. Joseph Rogers were cousins.

An old ranch with log buildings above the Alden place belonged to Alfred Turner, who also operated the store in Garo for many years after 1898. The Turner family came indirectly from Bordenville around 1890, about which more will be related later in the chapter.

The oldest ranch in the section—and one of the oldest in the park—was that of Adolph Guiraud. In 1863 he took up 160 acres on the South Fork of the South Platte at the water gap in Red Hill. Being the first rancher in the area, he acquired some of the most valuable water rights in the park; and, thus, his ranch became one of the most prominent. The old Guiraud Ditch comes out from behind Red Hill.

Guiraud, born in France in 1823, came to America when he was twenty-seven years old. His career as a wine importer and merchant took him first to New Orleans, then Cincinnati, and finally Kansas before he arrived in Denver in 1860. He was a merchant in Hamilton for two years before taking up the ranch at Garo.

Guiraud claimed South Park's first two permanent ditch rights for agricultural purposes in 1861 while he was in Hamilton, the first being to provide water to turn a wheel for churning his wife's butter, and the second to drain water from his hay meadow.

1864 found Guiraud in Denver operating a meat market, and in 1865 he had a store at Fairplay. Perhaps the Espinosa scare in 1863 followed by the visitation of his old acquaintance Jim Reynolds in 1864 had convinced him that life was more agreeable in town than on the farm. However, the Guirauds were back on the ranch in the winter of 1865-66 when Father Dyer stopped there one stormy night to rest a spell and to borrow a pony to continue on in the dark night.

Guiraud's ranch was only 640 acres by the time of his death in 1875. Apparently his interests lay with his old occupation as a merchant, for it was his widow who built the ranch holdings up to 5,000 acres. She raised large herds of cattle and big hay crops. Another of South Park's many legends is that $80,000 in gold was found hidden in Mrs. Guiraud's fruit cellar after her death.

Since 1941 the ranch has belonged to the McDowells and is now held in partnership with the Santa Maria Ranch. The McDowells' home is the old Guiraud house, though with its face lifted. The McDowells, in surveying their ranch, discovered that the last Guiraud owner had tended to put fences up wherever they suited his needs, and the ranch was not too accurately defined as a result.

The McDowells bought up the old townsite, just across the river from the ranchhouse, and removed the buildings. The old Garo schoolhouse, however, was moved to South Park City in Fairplay. This building was erected after 1879 when the arrival of the Denver, South Park, and Pacific Railway created the town of Garo (see Chapter VIII).

In 1880 the population of Garo reached as high as eighty. The store boosted the activity in Garo among the local ranchers. The store ledger for 1899-1900 (now at South Park City) has such names as W. P. McDowell, E. C. Guiraud, H. Chalmers, Chalmers and Galloway, and Will Arthur.

The Arthur family owned property north of the Guiraud Ranch on the DSP&P, it will be recalled. The Arthur ranch was established in 1874 by Englishman E. P. Arthur, who had owned a sheep ranch in Australia and another in Clear Creek County, Colorado, before he came to South Park. He built the ranch at Arthurs to 1,760 acres of good hay land and also developed the Platte Ranch to 2,200 acres. E. P. Arthur went into banking in Fairplay and Alma and then went to Cripple Creek.

On the west side of the South Platte and its tributaries, High Creek and Fourmile Creek, there are several outfits which were established in the early days. James F. F. Rushing mentioned in 1866 that "ranches thickened all the way" from the Salt Works to Fairplay. He also noted that there was "splendid duck-shooting" on the marshes beside the road.

In more recent times the foothills that front Buffalo Pass, Weston Pass, Breakneck Pass, and Brown's Pass along the Mosquito Range have been used by sheep for summer grazing. Ranchers then turn the animals onto their meadows in the park during the winter.

A little farther north early stock-raising ranches were established near Horseshoe Gulch and Fourmile Creek at Mullenville and at Pearts. In 1880 Mullenville, just two miles below the mining camp of Horseshoe, had a post office and a population of thirty. Four years later it was a stage station with a population of fifty, but there was no longer a post office, the office apparently having been absorbed by Horseshoe.

Pearts was a little east of Mullenville. Although it was principally a ranch belonging to a family of that name, Pearts also was a stage stop and became involved in the mining activity for a brief time.

A number of other properties in the vicinity of Fairplay appear on directories. Listed are a Bear Creek and Benkley's near Platte Station. Also Hubbard's, Hursley's Ranche, and Holly's Ranche are noted in 1896, as is a place called Guird's out of Como (apparently not connected with the Guiraud property which appears simultaneously). Also there are the Chile Springs near Como and in 1895 Centerville, seventeen miles east of Fairplay and four miles north.

The earliest reference to a ranch in the Fairplay area, though, dates back to July, 1860. It is a vague but colorful reference at best. Webster Anthony, in the company of two companions, was passing through South Park at that time on his way from Denver to Oro City by way of "Tarry-all" and what was apparently Mosquito Pass.

At the South Fork of the South Platte, during a summer storm, Anthony went to a "ranch" where he wanted to buy milk. The woman living there assured him that she had some to sell, but "By G-d, I guess the D-d thunder . . . soured it." So much for the earliest reports of ranching in the Fairplay area.

To complete the story of South Park's ranching, we must swing across the north end of the park to include the history of the activity in the Tarryall drainage basin. Although there were early ranches, such as the Links', all along the Tarryall northwest of Lake George by the 1870's, South Park's ranching on the Tarryall is limited geographically to the region north and west of Tarryall Reservoir.

A road as early as the 1860's ran from the site of Bordenville to Fairplay, partly for local miners but more especially for the through traffic which came up the lower Tarryall from Colorado City. In the late 1860's pioneer ranchers had also settled in the Tarryall bottom lands, as well as in the Kenosha Hill area and Lost Park.

In 1865 Timothy and Olney Borden settled at what was to become known as Bordenville. Timothy, born in New York State in 1826, came to the mines in Summit County in 1861 after living in Iowa for just a few years. Olney, the younger brother of Timothy, also ventured into mining near Golden prior to his coming to the park.

The Bordens built up their ranch to about 2,000 acres with excellent ditch rights, and they also operated a sawmill. They were among the most respected families in South Park, a reputation which was further enhanced when Olney married an "aristocratic" widow from St. Louis in 1880.

In addition to ranching and lumbering, the Bordens also operated a general merchandise store and a post office. The post office was a wing on the end of the white clapboard home which

250

still stands at Bordenville. The settlement at its peak had a population of about fifty with a stage stop, a blacksmith, and a mineral surveyor. Apparently traffic and the general mining excitement associated with the Leadville boom accounted for much of Bordenville's activity in the early 1880's, for postal service was discontinued in 1884, when the boom had quieted and the railroads were operating. By 1900 Bordenville was merely an aggregation of neighboring ranches without any town as such, and so it remains today.

A well-known and already frequently mentioned South Park family which lived at Bordenville was the Alfred Turners. Hiram Turner, originally from Canada and New York State, had been among the early miners at Breckenridge. His wife gave birth there to the first white child born in Summit County, and he was accordingly named Summit Turner. A second son of Hiram was Alfred. Before ranching at Bordenville, Alfred managed Leland Peabody's placer above Hamilton (see Chapter VII). From Bordenville the Turners returned to the Como area for a time and then moved to the ranch at Garo.

One of South Park's goriest and, yet, least known events occurred at Bordenville in 1895 when all three members of the school board were murdered in the schoolhouse. This school stood near a two-story ranchhouse now located at the junctions of the roads to Jefferson and Como, a little north of Bordenville.

According to a Denver *Daily News* report of the murder, the board had met on May 6 to try to formulate some means of forcing Benjamin Ratcliff to keep his children in school. However, according to local versions of the tale, Ben Ratcliff, whose wife had died (her grave is in the Bordenville cemetery with a marker dated 1882), had been living back in the hills causing some distasteful gossip, and the board was meeting to try to keep the children *out* of school.

Ratcliff rode to the school and shot all three—Samuel Taylor, Lincoln McCurdy, and George Wyatt. Taylor and McCurdy died instantly and Wyatt soon after. Ratcliff rode to Como and gave himself up; but he was tried, hanged at Canon City, and then

251

buried in the hills near Bordenville. The schoolhouse has since been moved.

Jefferson, seven miles north of the school, had threatened a necktie party for Ratcliff in the days immediately following the murder. However, cooler judgment prevailed.

Jefferson was to have its own scandal six years later. Uplide Vallie had a ranch a mile south of town, where he hired several hands to take care of the stock and haying since he worked in town as railroad station agent. One morning Vallie was found murdered in a field which he always cut across in the evening on his way home from the station. One of Vallie's hands was convicted of the murder. Vallie's widow was also accused as an accomplice, but she was acquitted.

Jefferson, happily, has been known better as a center of ranching than of crime. The town had been preceded by two other Jeffersons during the gold rush, the present-day Jefferson being established in 1879 when the Denver, South Park and Pacific narrow-gauge came through the park, it will be recalled.

Jefferson's first citizen was Willard Head, a Mormon originally from Nauvoo, Illinois. Head went to Utah as a child and became a teamster there in the 1850's. Running away from Utah, he came to Cherry Creek in 1858 but left for Nebraska until 1866. After freighting for a year between Julesburg and Denver, he ranched on Bear Creek and in Clear Creek County until 1873. Then he went to Bradford Junction (Conifer) for three years as a merchant. Head again freighted for a few years after 1876. When the Denver and South Park started up Platte Canyon, he become a tie contractor.

In 1879 he took up the ranch which is now the Johnston ranch at Jefferson. Getting there ahead of the railroad, he donated land from his ranch to the line for its right of way and opened a store. He also laid out the townsite of Jefferson on his property. His log house was the hotel and stage stop, from which Head ran a stage for a few years between the railroad and Swandyke over Georgia Pass. He was a county commissioner too in 1889. His original log house is now part of the large white home on the south side of town across the bridge over Jefferson Creek.

As the railroad was built, Jefferson became a tie shipping center. As early as 1880 Jones' Saw Mill and Webber's Saw Mill both were operating. Jones' mill, about thirteen miles east and six miles south of Red Hill, was still operating in 1896; and Webber's or "Old Saw Mill," seven miles due east of Arthurs, was in business well into the 1900's.

The population of Jefferson in 1880 was fifty-five, and there it has remained for the most part. By 1884 the town had two butchers, a saloon, a lumber mill, and a blacksmith, as well as the hotel and store. After 1890 the elder George Champion ran a store and the post office and was agent for the South Park Hay Company, a ranchers' cooperative. The association had a big hay barn on a railroad wye north of town.

Dairy farming around Jefferson was successful enough to warrant a cheese factory in the 1890's, and Champion was the agent for this venture, too. The factory operated for only a year or two, and afterward the building became the community center.

The schoolhouse which is now used as a church was the second school in Jefferson. The original building, across the creek and long vacated, burned in the 1960's.

Jefferson had a flurry of excitement in the 1940's when a well was drilled for oil north of town, and again in the 1950's when a gas well was drilled. However, nothing came of either, and Jefferson's economy remains based on the tons of hay which are produced annually on the neighboring ranches.

Except in the years 1892 and 1893, which were disastrously dry for miles around in the West, ranching in South Park has been almost always successful with sufficient quantities of hay for grazing as well as export. Even with the buying up of water rights and the building of reservoirs for the use of cities outside the park, there has been enough water for cattle and hay operations.

Antero Reservoir, named for a Ute chief who aided white settlers by controlling his tribe during Indian troubles, was finished in 1913. It was built by the Antero and Lost Park Company, which incorporated in 1907 for the purpose of building two reservoirs to supply water for irrigation between Denver and

Greeley, succeeding Denver's High Line Reservoir Company. Denver bought the water system in 1918 for the Denver Union Water Company.

The dam at Antero on the South Fork of the South Platte created a reservoir with a capacity of nearly eleven billion gallons. In the transfer of water rights to the owners of the reservoir, South Park ranchers gave up forty-five per cent of their total water rights—and not without a fight—but gained a steady supply of water through storage rights which allowed use of about one-fourth of the lake's capacity. Since 1952 Colorado Springs also has stored Blue River water in Antero Reservoir in a diversion project which brings Western Slope water through Hoosier Pass to Montgomery Dam and across South Park to Colorado Springs.

The Elevenmile Canyon Reservoir, built by Denver in 1931, again dammed the South Fork of the South Platte. Its capacity is over twenty-six billion gallons. In 1966 Colorado Springs began to use this reservoir also for storage of Western Slope water from the Homestake Project.

Tarryall Reservoir is a Colorado Game, Fish, and Parks Department project, used for trout spawning.

Despite the arguments of the reservoir builders, South Park's agriculture has been significantly changed since they came in. A study by Roy Davidson has indicated that whereas there were 213 operators irrigating fields in 1920, there were only seventy-five in 1940. The miles of ditches dropped from 506 to 300 in the same period, and acres under irrigation from 50,000 to 40,000.

These figures suggest other changes besides the building of the reservoirs, however. First, the ranches passed to fewer hands. Second, there have been changes in the purposes to which the land was put.

For example, between 1883 and 1928 the number of sheep grazed in South Park increased four times, but the figure is now back down closer to the earlier period. Now, with about 15,000 sheep South Park is exceeded by one-third of the state's counties in sheep production. Its cattle herds are estimated at around 26,000 head, a number which is more than equalled by half of Colorado's counties.

But as a hay producer, Park County is exceeded only by Jackson County in Colorado. The park is classified today by the Department of Agriculture as grazing land with its principal crop range grass. Of this, only 200 acres of alfalfa hay were harvested in 1961 as compared with 34,000 acres of wild hay.

However, with the combined losses of irreplaceable water rights, much of the mining activity, and railroad tax revenues in the twentieth century, South Park has often felt that its hands were tied in terms of future development. With the exception of present-day tourists and outdoorsmen, the economy of the park rests almost exclusively on ranching. Whereas the state's average income per family was $5,780 in 1960, Park County's average was $4,900.

Even at the height of the park's economy, schools were minimal, and it has been a struggle to make them something more. There were just twenty-six schools (almost all one-room) scattered over the vast park and its surrounding mountains in 1893 in an area larger than the state of Rhode Island. The three existing libraries had a total of 450 volumes.

However, by the turn of the century improvements were being brought about. Many of the school terms had been extended from three to five or six months, and the state course of study was being followed. Several "poor log buildings" had been replaced by "commodious, well-ventilated buildings."

In order to upgrade education in recent years, South Park's schools have been consolidated. The paradoxical solution was to have just one school district with all of the students traveling to Fairplay, where the new South Park Junior-Senior High School was built in 1963.

The park has fought a similar battle for adequate medical facilities. For about fifty years Fairplay had a hospital in a structure that had previously been the local Ku Klux Klan headquarters. Eventually it was condemned as a firetrap. After years of citizen effort, a new hospital which also serves as a nursing home was built in the 1970's.

Although South Park's low, year-round population has limited some public services in the past, the rapid growth of the Denver metropolitan area during the 1970's affected the park's life. Along with sightseers and weekenders came land developers, bulldozers, and increased commerce. Also, increases in the price of gold and silver excited interest in mining again. Many of the recent operations have been shoestring operations, but others, like the work at London Mountain, have brought large investors to South Park's mines once more. With the value of minerals skyrocketing, mining companies could risk heavy expenditures to process low-grade ores that were bypassed a century ago.

Despite changes which have come to South Park, one still can stand on Wilkerson Pass or Kenosha Pass and visualize the long succession of those who have known the beautiful land below. Indians, explorers, trappers, miners, railroaders, ranchers, bad men (and racy women), statesmen, tourists—all came, and none found South Park wanting.

Bayou Salado, as infinite in variety and breadth as man's longings.

Acknowledgments

My great appreciation is owed to a number of people who have shared information and pictures for use in this book. Among them are Vaun Benjamin, Dorothy Champion Fahrion, Mrs. E. W. Hanlin, Abby Kernochan, Beth Kraig, John J. Lipsey, Carl Mathews, Ray Moore, Richard M. Pearl, Leon Snyder, Frank Turner, and George White. Also, the many people who originally contributed photographs to the South Park City collection are especially thanked for the materials which were used in this book.

In addition, I wish to recognize the invaluable sources of material generously made available to researchers through the Denver Public Library's Western History Department and the Library of the State Historical Society of Colorado. These collections have been drawn upon extensively and always with the efficient and cooperative help of the fine staffs of these libraries.

Finally, Mike Walton and Darrell Porter of Darrell Porter Photography should be cited for their generous efforts in assisting an amateur shutter-bug to obtain adequate photographic prints of scenes which were not otherwise available. They performed darkroom wonders with my snapshots.

Bibliography

Anthony, Webster D. "Journal of a Trip from Denver to Oro City in 1860," *Colorado Magazine*, XI (November 1934), 228-237.

Arnold, Frazer. "Samuel Hartsel," *Colorado Magazine*, XIX (May 1942), 99-101.

Bair, Everett. *This Will Be an Empire*. New York, 1959.

Bergh, Abraham. Personal statement. Bancroft manuscript, Norlin Library, University of Colorado, 1886. (Photostat.)

Bird, Horace A. *History of a Line*. New York, 1889.

Blake, Forrester. *Johnny Christmas*. New York, 1948.

Boyles, Samuel. *A Summer Vacation in the Parks and Mountains of Colorado*. Boston, 1869.

Brewer, William Henry. *Rocky Mountain Letters, 1869*. Denver, 1930.

Burt, S. W., and E. L. Berthoud. *The Rocky Mountain Gold Regions*. Denver, 1962. (First published in 1861: Denver.)

Cafky, Morris. *Colorado Midland*. Denver, 1965.

Carroll, Richard. "Mary Nash Mear," *Colorado Magazine*, XI (November 1934), 216-217.

Champion, George W. "Remembrances of South Park," *Colorado Magazine*, XL (January 1963), 19-31.

Chandler, Allison. "The Story of Como and King Park, Colorado," *Denver Westerners' Monthly Roundup*, XIX (February 1963), 4.

Cheetham, Francis T., "Early Settlements," *Colorado Magazine*, V (February 1928), 1-8.

Chittenden, H. M. *The American Fur Trade in the Far West,* Vol. II. New York, 1902.

Colorado Geological Survey. *Geology and Ore Deposits of the Alma District.* Bulletin No. 3. Denver, 1912.

————————————. *Geology of the Tarryall District.* Bulletin No. 31. Denver, 1925.

Colwell, Raymond Gardner. "Rustlers and Recluses," *The Westerners' Denver Posse Brand Book.* Denver, 1956.

Como Iron, Coal, and Land Company. *Prospectus, Charter, and By-laws.* N.p., n.d.

Davidson, Roy Allyn. "A History of Park County, Colorado." Unpublished Master's thesis, University of Denver, 1940.

Douthit, George. "Dear Mr. Leaper," Colorado Springs *Gazette Telegraph, Leisuretime Magazine,* September 19, 1964, 16-17.

Drannan, William F. *Thirty-one Years on the Plains and in the Mountains.* N.p., n.d.

Dyer, John L. *The Snow-Shoe Itinerant.* Cincinnati, Ohio, 1890.

Ecke, Dean H., and Clifford W. Johnson. "Plague in Park County," *Plague in Colorado and Texas.* U.S. Public Health Service Publication No. 210. Washington, 1952.

Epperson, Harry A. *Colorado as I Saw It.* Kaysville, Utah, 1944.

Everett, George G. and Wendell F. Hutchinson. *Under the Angel of Shavano.* Denver, 1963.

Fenwick, Robert W. "Light on the Mystery of Silver Heels," Denver *Post, Empire Magazine,* November 3, 1963, 16-21.

Fisher, J. R. *Camping in the Rocky Mountains.* Papers read before the Ladies' Aid Society of the Second Presbyterian Church, Jersey City, New Jersey, 1880.

Flynn, Norma Louise. "Early Mining Camps of South Park," *The Westerners' Denver Posse Brand Book.* Denver, 1952.

————————————. "History of the Famous Mosquito Pass," *The Westerners' Denver Posse Brand Book.* Denver, 1959.

————————————. "South Park: Seventy-five Years of its History." Unpublished Master's thesis, University of Denver, 1947.

Fossett, Frank. *Colorado, Its Gold and Silver Mines.* New York, 1880.

George, R. D., *et al. Mineral Waters of Colorado*. Colorado Geological Survey Bulletin No. 11. Denver, 1920.

Giddens, Paul H. "Letters of S. Newton Pettis," *Colorado Magazine*, XV (January 1938), 3-14.

Hafen, LeRoy R. "The Bean-Sinclair Party of Rocky Mountain Trappers," *Colorado Magazine*, XXXI (July 1954), 161-171.

Hafen, LeRoy R. "Seventy Years Ago—Recollections of a Trip through the Colorado Mountains with the Colfax Party in 1868," as told by Mrs. Frank Hall, *Colorado Magazine*, XV (September 1938), 161-168.

Hall, Frank. *History of the State of Colorado*, Vols. I, II, and IV. Chicago, 1889.

Hedges, William Hawkins. *Pikes Peak . . . or Busted!* ed. Herbert O. Brayer. Evanston, Illinois, 1954.

Hillhouse, J. N. "The Sheldon Jackson Memorial Church at Fairplay," *Colorado Magazine*, XXIII (September 1946), 5.

Jack, John G. *Pikes Peak, Plum Creek and South Platte Forest Reserve*. Washington, 1900.

Jackson, William Henry. *Time Exposure: the Autobiography of William Henry Jackson*. New York, 1940.

Janes, Addison M., comp. *The Incorporation and Ordinances of South Park City as Adopted Since Incorporation of the Town, March 26, 1869 to May 15, 1869*. N.p., 1869.

Keeton, Elsie. "The Story of Dead Man's Canon and the Espinosas," *Colorado Magazine*, VII (January 1931), 34.

Kindig, R. H., Haley, E. J., and M. C. Poor. *Denver, South Park and Pacific Pictorial Supplement*. Denver, 1959.

Latham, H. *Trans-Missouri Stock Raising*. Omaha, 1871.

Lathrop, G. A. *Little Engines and Big Men*. Caldwell, Idaho, 1954.

Legard, A. B. *Colorado*. London, 1872.

Lipsey, John J. "The Bayou Salade: South Park," *The Westerners' Denver Posse Brand Book*. Denver, 1946.

Mumey, Nolie. *Early Mining Laws of Buckskin Joe, 1859*. Boulder, Colorado, 1961.

.... *History and Legal Proceedings of Buckskin Joe, 1859-1862*. Boulder, Colorado, 1961.

Ormes, Robert M. *Railroads and the Rockies*. Denver, 1963.

Parkhill, Forbes. *The Law Goes West*. Denver, 1956.

Paul, Rodman W. *Mining Frontiers of the Far West, 1848-1880*. New York, 1963.

Pile, George S. "A Toll Road into South Park," *Colorado Magazine*, XXVII (July 1950), 192-198.

Pine, George W. *Beyond the West*. Utica, New York, 1870.

Poor, M. C. *Denver, South Park and Pacific*. Denver, 1949.

Post Route Maps of the State of Colorado. 1877, 1906.

Preuss, Charles. *Exploring with Fremont*, ed. and trans. Erwin G. and Elisabeth K. Gudde. Norman, Oklahoma, 1958.

Quaife, Milo Milton, ed. *The Southwestern Expedition of Zebulon M. Pike*. Chicago, 1925.

Richie, Eleanor Louise. "Spanish Relations with the Yuta Indians, 1680-1822." Unpublished Master's thesis, University of Denver, 1932.

Ridgway, Arthur. "The Mission of Colorado Toll Roads," *Colorado Magazine*, IX (September 1932), 161.

Robison, Lyman. Personal statement. Bancroft manuscript, Norlin Library, University of Colorado, 1885. (Photostat.)

Rudolph, Gerald E. "The Chinese in Colorado, 1869-1911." Unpublished Master's thesis, University of Denver, 1964.

Ruxton, George Frederick. *Adventures in Mexico and the Rocky Mountains*. New York, 1848.

.... *Life in the Far West*, ed. LeRoy R. Hafen. Norman, Oklahoma, 1951.

Sage, Rufus B. "Letters and Scenes in the Rocky Mountains, 1836-1847," *The Far West and the Rockies Historical Series*, Vol. V, ed. LeRoy R. and Ann W. Hafen. Glendale, California, 1954.

Sanford, Albert B. "Mountain Staging in Colorado," *Colorado Magazine*, IX (March 1932), 66.

Schenck, Annie B. "Camping Vacation, 1871," ed. Jack D. Filipiak, *Colorado Magazine*, (Summer 1965), 185-215.

Spiva, Agnes Elizabeth. "Utes in Colorado, 1863-1880." Unpublished Master's thesis, University of Colorado, 1929.

Sprague, Marshall. *The Great Gates: The Story of the Rocky Mountain Passes*. Boston and Toronto, 1964.

.... *Newport in the Rockies*. Denver, 1961.

Stark, J. T., *et al. Geology and Origin of South Park Colorado.* New York, 1949.

Steinel, Alvin Theodore. *History of Agriculture in Colorado.* Ft. Collins, Colorado, 1926.

Taylor, Bayard. *Colorado: A Summer Trip.* New York, 1867.

Teller, Henry M. Papers. Norlin Library, University of Colorado.

Thwaite, Reuben Gold, ed. *Thwaite's Early Western Travels, 1748-1846,* Vols. XV, XVI, XVIII. Cleveland, 1907.

United Mining District Miners' Convention. Minutes. 1860.

University of Denver Anthropology Department. *Archeological Survey of South Park, Colorado.* Archeological series, papers 1-6, 1934-1946.

Weimer, Robert J., and John D. Haun, ed. *Guide to the Geology of Colorado.* Denver, 1960.

Whitford, William Clarke. *Colorado Volunteers in the Civil War.* Boulder, Colorado, 1963. (First published in 1906: Denver.)

Witter, Clara Viali (Colfax). *Pioneer Life.* N.p., n.d.

Woodward, Patrick Henry. *Guarding the Mails.* Hartford, Connecticut, 1881.

Index

263

264

266

269

Machebeuf, Father Joseph, 100
MacKay, Henry, 99
MacMillan, Samuel, 148
Magnolia Mill, 109
Mahoneyville, Colo., 146
Major, Alexander, 68, 217
Mandan Indians, 54
Manitou Springs, 19, 59, 176, 202
Manoa, Colo., 246
Masons, 30
Masonic Lodge, 153
Mathews, Albert E., 73
Mattias (Pueblo Indian), 60
Mayer, Col. Frank, 161
Mayol, Mrs. Frank (married Samuel Hartsel), 219
McClelland, William, 77, 117-8, 128, 151
McCurdy, Lincoln, 251
McDannald, A. T. "Cap," 221
McDowell Ranch (W. P. McDowell), 35, 222, 232, 248
McFarland (hanged at Tarryall), 73
McFee, "Old Bill," 197
McFerran, J. H. B., 147
McGee, Jim, 150
McLaughlin, Dan, 110, 118-9
McLaughlin, Matthew (stage line), 117, 126, 128, 150, 152, 154, 235
McLean (teacher at Fairplay), 110
McNab (a Moose Mine owner), 120
McQuaid, Bernard, 213
McQuaid, Delia, 213
McQuaid, Mrs. Thomas (Mildred Hall), 24, 212-3
McQuaid, Thomas, 213
Meek, "Colonel" Joseph, 56-7
Meeker massacre, 30
Meeker, Nathan C., 214-5
Metcalf (shot by Espinosas), 116
Methodist Church, 100, 109, 124, 153, 155
Meyers, Augustus R., 123
Michigan Creek, 60, 74, 80
Michigan House, 80, 118
Michigan Siding, 171
Middle Park, 14, 25, 29, 58-60
Miner's Record, 98, 104, 108
Missouri Fur Co., 55
Moffat, David H., 165, 169
Monarch Pass, 26

Montezuma Mine, 154
Montgomery, Colo., 65, 78, *81-5, 90*, 100, 103-5, 108-12, 118, 121-2, 126, *131*
Montgomery Dam, *85*, 109, 122, 254
Montgomery Gulch, 163
Montgomery Falls, 76, *84*, 122
Moore Mining and Smelting Co., 124
Moore, Ray, 221
Moose Mine (Moose Mining Co.), *86-7*, 120-3, 196
Morgan, Frank, 176
Morose, Martin, 246
Morrison, Colo., 68, 169-70
Mosquito Creek (Gulch), *41*, 107, 123, 126-7, 145, 175, 196, 198
Mosquito Mining District (Mosquito), *42, 48*, 104-8, 127-8, 145-6, 173, 196-7; *see also* Sterling
Mosquito Pass, 15, 26, *42, 44*, 75, 107-8, 127-8, 145-6, 150, 172, 250
Mosquito Pass Wagon Road Co., 128, 145, 159
Mosquito Range, 15-6, 19, *44*, 80, 92, 107, 150, 201-2
Mosquito Range and Leadville Tunnel and Mining Co., 196
Mt. Bross, 15, *38, 86*, 120, 122-3, 127, *138*
Mt. Cameron, 15, *39*, 108
Mt. Democrat, 15
Mt. Evans, *34*
Mt. Lincoln, 15, *81, 85-6*, 111-2, 120-2, 154, 196
Mount Lincoln News, 124, 155
Mt. Lincoln Smelting Works, 121
Mt. Sheridan, 92, *94*, 147, 150, 198
Mt. Sherman, 15, *91, 92*, 146, 148
Mt. Silverheels, 15, 50, 74, 102, 163, *232*
Mt. Vernon Canyon, 67
Moynahan, James, 124-5
Mudsill, Colo., 148, 199
Mudsill Mine, 148, 199
Mullen (discoverer of the Sacramento), 146
Mullenville, Colo., 249
Mulock, Ira, 242-3
Murdock, Hugh, 118, 152, 154

272

273

274

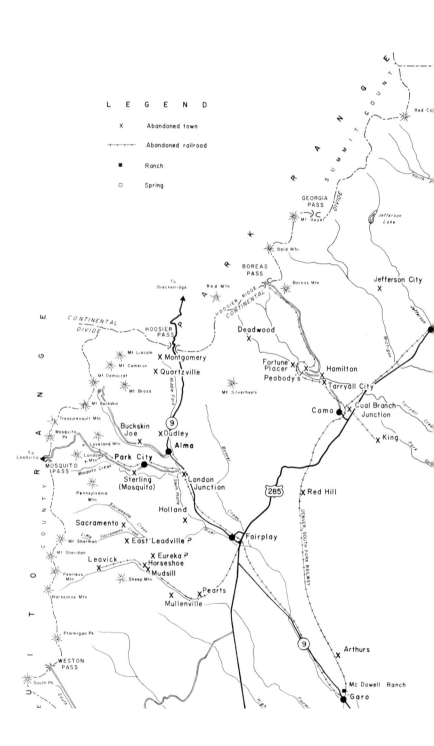

LEGEND

X   Abandoned town

+—+—+   Abandoned railroad

■   Ranch

□   Spring

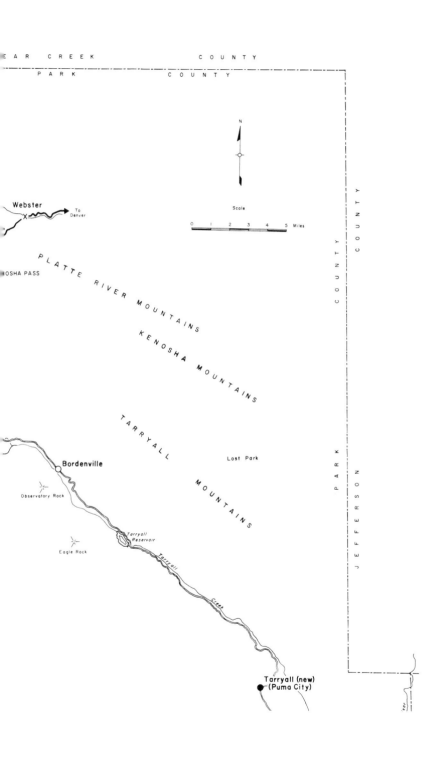

E A R   C R E E K   C O U N T Y

P A R K   C O U N T Y

N

Scale

0   1   2   3   4   5   Miles

Webster
X
To Denver

P L A T T E   R I V E R   M O U N T A I N S

OSHA PASS

K E N O S H A   M O U N T A I N S

T A R R Y A L L

Bordenville

Observatory Rock

M O U N T A I N S

Lost Park

Eagle Rock

Tarryall Reservoir

Tarryall

Creek

P A R K   C O U N T Y

J E F F E R S O N   C O U N T Y

Tarryall (new)
(Puma City)

ver

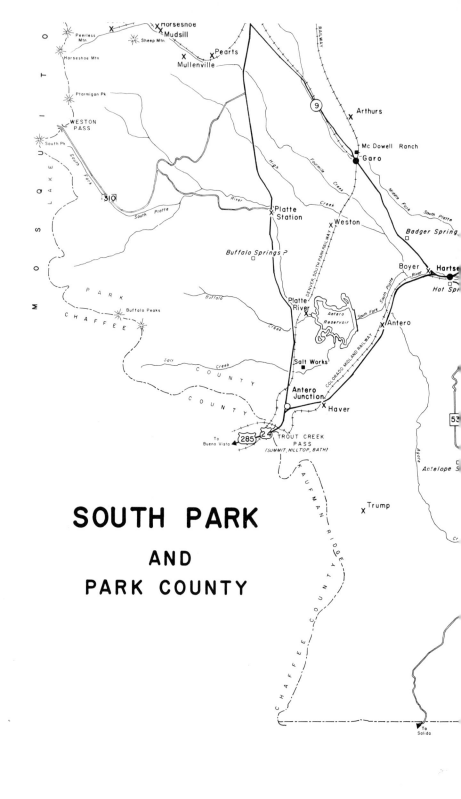

Peerless Mtn · ✦ X ✦ X Horseshoe Mudsill
Sheep Mtn

Horseshoe Mtn

X Pearts

X Mullenville

RAILWAY

Ptarmigan Pk ✦

9 Arthurs

WESTON PASS

Mc Dowell Ranch

South Pk

Garo

South Fork

South Platte River

310

South Platte

Platte Station

High

Fourmile Creek

Middle Fork

South Platte

X Weston

Badger Spring

Creek

DENVER, SOUTH PARK RAILWAY

Buffalo Springs ?

Boyer River

Hartse

Hot Spr

PARK

Buffalo

Platte River

Antero Reservoir

South Fork

South Platte

CHAFFEE

Buffalo Peaks ✦

Creek

X Antero

COUNTY

Salt Creek

Salt Works

COLORADO MIDLAND RAILWAY

COUNTY

Antero Junction

X Haver

53

285

TROUT CREEK PASS
(SUMMIT, HILLTOP, BATH)

To Bueno Vista

Agate

Antelope S

KAUFMAN RIDGE

X Trump

SOUTH PARK

AND

PARK COUNTY

CHAFFEE COUNTY

To Salida

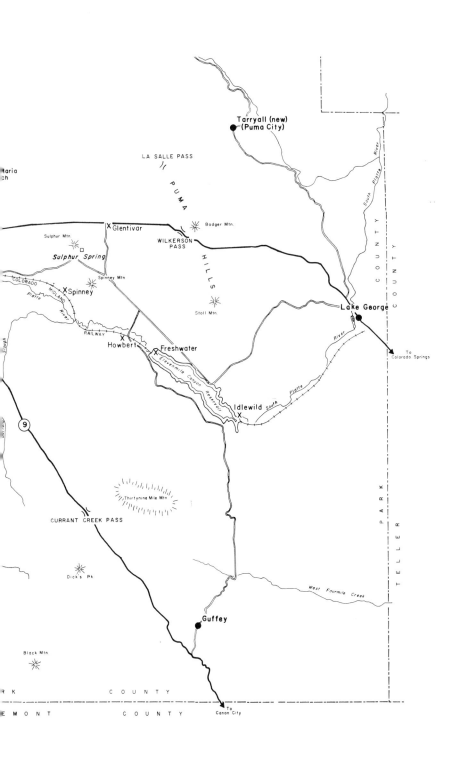